AIRPORTS IN THE CARIBBEAN

Books LLC®, Reference Series, Memphis, USA, 2011. ISBN: 9781155980393. www.booksllc.net. Copyright: http://creativecommons.org/licenses/by-sa/3.0/deed.en

Table of Contents

Airports in Aruba
List of airports in Aruba 2
Queen Beatrix International Airport ... 2

Airports in Barbados
Grantley Adams International Airport 3
List of airports in Barbados 6

Airports in Bermuda
L.F. Wade International Airport 6
List of airports in Bermuda 8

Airports in Cuba
Abel Santamaría Airport 8
Alberto Delgado Airport 8
Antonio Maceo Airport 8
Carlos Manuel de Céspedes Airport ... 9
Cayo Coco Airport 9
Ciudad Libertad Airport 9
ECASA 9
Florida Airport (Cuba) 9
Frank País Airport 10
Gustavo Rizo Airport 10
Hermanos Ameijeiras Airport 10
Ignacio Agramonte International Airport 10
Jaime González Airport 11
Jardines del Rey Airport 11
Joaquín de Agüero Airport................ 11
José Martí International Airport 11
Juan Gualberto Gómez Airport 13
Kawama Airport 14
La Coloma Airport 14
Las Brujas Airport (Cuba) 14
Leeward Point Field 15
List of airports in Cuba 15
Mariana Grajales Airport 15
Máximo Gómez Airport 15
Nicaro Airport 15
Orestes Acosta Airport 15
Pinar del Río Airport 16
Playa Baracoa Airport 16
Rafael Cabrera Airport 16
Rafael Pérez Airport 16
San Antonio de los Baños Air Base .. 16
San Nicolás de Bari Airport 17

Sancti Spíritus Airport 17
Sierra Maestra Airport 17
Siguanea Airport 17
Vilo Acuña Airport 17

Airports in Curaçao
Hato International Airport 18

Airports in Guadeloupe
List of airports in Guadeloupe 19
Marie-Galante Airport 19
Pointe-à-Pitre International Airport .. 19

Airports in Martinique
List of airports in Martinique 19
Martinique Aimé Césaire International Airport 20

Airports in Saba
Juancho E. Yrausquin Airport 20

Airports in Saint Barthélemy
Gustaf III Airport 21
List of airports in Saint Barthélemy .. 21

Airports in Saint Eustatius
F.D. Roosevelt Airport 22

Airports in Saint Pierre and Miquelon
List of airports in Saint Pierre and Miquelon 22
Miquelon Airport 22
Saint-Pierre Airport 23

Airports in Saint Vincent and the Grenadines
Argyle International Airport 23
Canouan Airport 24
E. T. Joshua Airport 24
J. F. Mitchell Airport 24
List of airports in Saint Vincent and the Grenadines 24
Mustique Airport 24
Union Island Airport 24

Airports in Sint Maarten
List of airports in Saint Martin 25
Princess Juliana International Airport 25

Airports in the Bahamas
Andros Town International Airport .. 27
Arthur's Town Airport 27
Chub Cay International Airport 27
Clarence A. Bain Airport 27
Colonel Hill Airport 27
Congo Town Airport 27
Deadman's Cay Airport 27
Duncan Town Airport 28
Exuma International Airport 28
George Town Airport 28
Governor's Harbour Airport 28
Grand Bahama International Airport 28
Great Harbour Cay Airport 29
Inagua Airport 29
List of airports in the Bahamas 29
Lynden Pindling International Airport 30
Marsh Harbour Airport 30
Mayaguana Airport 31
New Bight Airport 31
Norman's Cay Airport 31
North Eleuthera Airport 31
Port Nelson Airport 31
Rock Sound International Airport 31
San Andros Airport 31
San Salvador Airport 32
Sandy Point Airport 32
South Bimini Airport 32
Spanish Cay Airport 32
Spring Point Airport 32
Staniel Cay Airport 33
Stella Maris Airport 33
Treasure Cay Airport 33
West End Airport 33

Airports in the Caribbean
Flamingo International Airport 33
List of airports in the Caribbean 36
List of airports in the Netherlands Antilles 36

2 - Introduction

List of busiest airports in Latin America by passenger traffic 36
List of the busiest airports in South America 36
Airports in the Collectivity of Saint Martin
L'Espérance Airport 37

Introduction

Purchase of this book entitles you to a free trial membership in the publisher's book club at www.booksllc.net. (Time limited offer.) Simply enter the barcode number from the back cover onto the membership form. The book club entitles you to select from hundreds of thousands of books at no additional charge. You can also download a digital copy of this and related books to read on the go. Simply enter the title or subject onto the search form to find them.

Each chapter in this book ends with a URL to a hyperlinked online version. Type the URL exactly as it appears. If you change the URL's capitalization it won't work. Use the online version to access related pages, websites, footnotes, tables, color photos, updates. Click the version history tab to see the chapter's contributors. Click the edit link to suggest changes.

A large and diverse editor base collaboratively wrote the book, not a single author. After a long process of discussion and debate, the chapters gradually took on a neutral point of view reached through consensus. Additional editors expanded and contributed to chapters striving to achieve balance and comprehensive coverage. This reduced the regional or cultural bias found in many other books and provided access and breadth on subject matter otherwise little documented.

List of airports in Aruba

This is a **list of airports in Aruba**.

Source (edited): "http://en.wikipedia. org/wiki/List_of_airports_in_Aruba"

Queen Beatrix International Airport

Queen Beatrix International Airport (IATA: **AUA**, ICAO: **TNCA**) (Papiamento: *Aeropuerto Internacional Reina Beatrix*), in Oranjestad, Aruba, is an aviation facility. It has flight services to the United States, most countries in the Caribbean, the northern coastal countries of South America, Canada and some parts of Europe, notably the Netherlands. It was named after Queen Beatrix of the Netherlands, the head of state of Aruba.

This airport used to serve as the hub for bankrupt airline Air Aruba, which was for many years an international airline. Before Aruba's separation from the Netherlands Antilles in 1986 it was also one of three hubs for Air ALM. The airport has a new airline, Tiara Air.

The airport offers US Border Preclearance facilities.

A terminal for private aircraft opened in 2007.

Airlines and destinations

A Continental Airlines Boeing 737-800 landing

US Airways Boeing 757 departing

World War II

During World War II the airport was used by the United States Army Air Force Sixth Air Force defending Caribbean shipping and the Panama Canal against German submarines. Flying units assigned to the airfield were:

- 59th Bombardment Squadron (9th Bombardment Group) 14 January-24 September 1942 (A-20 Havoc)
- 12th Bombardment Squadron (25th Bombardment Group) 10 October 1942–23 November 1943 (B-18 Bolo)
- 22d Fighter Squadron (36th Fighter Group) 2 September 1942-April 1943 (P-40 Warhawk)
- 32d Fighter Squadron (Antilles Air Command) 9 March 1943-March 1944 (P-40 Warhawk)

Incidents and Accidents

- 13 January 2010, an Arkefly Boeing 767-300 PH-AHQ operating flight OR361 from Amsterdam Schiphol Airport to **Aruba Airport** declared an emergency after a man who claimed to have a bomb on board insued a struggle with the flight crew, the aircraft made an emergency Landing at Shannon Airport. Gardai stormed the plane and arrested the man, where he was taken to Shannon Garda station. A passenger having had surgery earlier the month before collapsed in the terminal while waiting for the continuation of the flight and had to be taken to a local hospital. The repacment aircraft PH-AHY also a Boeing 767-300 continued the flight to **Aruba**.

Source (edited): "http://en.wikipedia.org/wiki/Queen_Beatrix_International_Airport"

Grantley Adams International Airport

The Airport

Grantley Adams International Airport (GAIA), (IATA: **BGI**, ICAO: **TBPB**) is found in Seawell, Christ Church on the island of Barbados. The former name of the airport was **Seawell Airport** before being dedicated in honour of the first Premier of Barbados, Sir Grantley Herbert Adams in 1976. The airport's timezone is GMT –4, and is located in World Area Code region #246 (by the U.S. Department of Transportation). GAIA is the only designated port of entry for persons arriving and departing by air in Barbados.

Grantley Adams Airport has direct service to destinations in the United States, Canada, Central America, South America and Europe and operates as a major gateway to the Eastern Caribbean. The airport is a second hub for Leeward Islands Air Transport (LIAT), and hub for new LCC, REDjet. The airport is an important air-link for cruise lines departing and arriving to Bridgetown, and a base of operations for the Regional Security System (RSS).

Overview and geography

The Grantley Adams International Airport lies 12.9 km (8 mi.) from the centre of the capital city Bridgetown, in an area officially known as Seawell. This is contrary to most informational services stating the airport as being located inside the capital city.

The terrain around the airport is relatively flat and quite suburban. The airport lies in the south-eastern portion of parish of Christ Church, close to the southern tip of the entire island. The airport is provided with easy access to the ABC Highway/highway 7 heading towards the capital and locations to the north and west coast of the island.

The Grantley Adams Airport also serves as the main air-transportation hub for the Eastern Caribbean. The airport has recently undergone a multi-phase US$100 million upgrade and expansion by the government, which added a brand new arrivals hall adjacent to the prior arrivals/departures terminals. Construction was made slightly more complicated due to the fact that the airport has to remain open for up to 16 hours per day. The Airport's current infrastructure is supposed to meet the needs of Barbados until at least 2015. The phase III construction project, which is yet to be completed will see changes made to the airplane parking configuration at the airport.

Currently parking is available outside the airport at a rate of Bds$2.00 per hour or a maximum rate Bds$12.00 daily.

Runway and taxiways

The Airport has a single east-westerly runway, connected by five taxiway intersections with the aircraft parking area which is adjacent to the main terminals. As a result of the earths' tradewinds that blow from the Atlantic Ocean across Barbados from the east, all planes usually land and take-off in an easterly direction. This results in a typical flight path for arriving aircraft along the west coast of Barbados, while departing flights usually fly along the east coast of the island. On relatively rare but not uncommon occurrences, some weather disturbances, such as passing hurricanes or tropical systems, may cause planes to take off or land in a westerly direction such as on 29 August 2010.

History

Former Seawell Airport during the 1960s.

Air transportation at the site of present day airport, then known as *Seawell Airport*, goes back as far as the late 1930s. In 1939 a plane from the Royal Netherlands Airlines landed on the airport site. At the time there was merely a grassy strip as the runway. The strip was paved some time later and in 1949 the first Terminal building was built on the site, to replace a shed that was being used until then. This ushered in the Airport being formally known as the *Seawell Airport*.

During the 1960s the eastern flight-range just south-east of the airport became known as Paragon. This area of the airport became the initial base of a *High Altitude Research Project* known as Project HARP, Project HARP was jointly sponsored by McGill University in Canada and the United States military.

In 1983, the U.S.-sponsored invasion of Grenada prompted the United States to form yet another agreement with Barbados. As part of the deal, the U.S. expanded a part of the current airport infrastructure. This prepared the Grantley Adams Airport to be used as a base. The U.S. military oversaw the upgrading of the Airport runway in order for it to handle larger U.S. military aircraft on their way to neighbouring Grenada. As part of the plan to maintain lasting stability in Grenada, the United States also assisted in the establishment of the Regional Security System (RSS) at the eastern Grantley Adams airport flightrage. The R.S.S. was (and still is) a security unit focused on providing security for the Eastern Caribbean.

The Grantley Adams International Airport, as it is known today, handles most large aircraft including Boeing 747s. The airport was also one of the few destinations in the world where British Airways' Concorde aircraft made regularly scheduled flights, and also for repairs, before Concorde was retired. Concorde typically flew to Barbados during the busy UK-Barbados winter season. The flight time of Concorde from the United Kingdom to Barbados was less than 4 hours.

2000-2006 Expansion project

Renovated terminal

Since the Grantley Adams International Airport had become a relatively busy airport for such a small island, and based on the fact that future air traffic to the facilities is expected to increase, the Government of Barbados commenced a US$100 million programme to revamp the Airport's current infrastructure.

Phase I, which is now complete, saw an upgrading of the Runways, taxiways, parking aprons, and approach lighting. This phase also included the Government of Barbados acquiring private land adjacent to the landing strip in order to bring the airport into compliance with new international aviation regulations.

Phase II (also complete), included adding a brand new arrivals terminal adjacent to the current building; moving arrivals from the current terminal, renovating the current terminal as a departures facility, and bringing the airport infrastructure current for the new millennium.

2006-beyond expansion

On 1 June 2007, the Bds$1.7 million Club Caribbean Executive Lounge and Business Centre was opened as an added amenity for business travellers. The centre contains 5,000 Sq. ft. and is located on the mezzanine level. The centre is meant to be used by special customers of several airlines at the terminal.

The Phase III expansion planned had to wait until the completion of the 2007 Cricket World Cup, it envisions the addition of new airport terminal Jetway (gates), new spacious departure lounges much closer to the airplanes and air bridges to make connections at the facility much easier. Also nearing completion is the expanded duty free shopping area and restaurants for travellers. In 2010 airport authorities stated that traffic to the airport was up 58% and that a 20-25 year plan was being formed for the facility including an addition to the current taxiway and renovation of the cargo facilities up to international standards.

New Arrivals building

After the expansion project, the airport's Arrivals facility was moved to a separate brand-new 70,000 square foot building adjacent to the previous structure. This allowed the Departures area to occupy much of the previous shared structure. The new arrivals terminal was built with five large baggage carousels. Along with a number of customs and immigration windows for processing travellers.

Terminals, airlines and destinations

The Sir Grantley Adams International Airport has two terminal buildings designed to appear to be one single continuous structure. The first structure and oldest is the current departures terminal. This terminal stretches from gates 11–13. Prior to the 2000-2006 expansion project, the original single terminal building housed both the arrivals and departures facilities. The former layout was divided in two with a few duty free shops and an open-air area in the middle of the airport with trees and other greenery which was open to both halves of the terminal. The new translucent membrane that towers over the airport shows the place where the old terminal was split in two. Additionally the same membrane tent design over the building also covers the gap between the old and new terminal and gives the appearance of both buildings being a single long building. The new terminal spans gates 1–10

Passenger

The following airlines serve the following destinations:

REDjet

In 2010, a private sector envoy announced an intention to base a start-up airline at the Sir Grantley Adams International Airport. The name of the parent company is *AIRONE Ventures Limited (AVL)*, and the air venture will seek to form "the Caribbean's first low-cost carrier". The envoy, mainly from Ireland, had initially attempted to begin operations from Jamaica however, Jamaican aviation authorities reportedly rejected their application for licenses. Following this, the envoy shifted focus basing operations from Barbados. The partnership is said to have begun as a partnership of a handful of business executives from Jamaica-based Digicel. Digicel is also said to be a major player in the marketing regime/scheme for the airline. The airline have began seeking approval of U.S. authorities to fly to that market in early 2010 and originally projected to commence operations on December 1, 2010. After 3 months of dedicated regional service the airline would then proceed with plans to service Fort Lauderdale and other US key destinations from the Caribbean. On October 16, 2010 Airone Ventures Ltd. launched their airline brand REDjet, at the Sir Lloyd Erskine Sandiford Conference and Culture Centre formerly known as Sherbourne Centre. On December 10, the airline's first (of two) introductory McDonnell Douglas MD-82aircraft named 'Jacqualicious' after an employee, was delivered to REDjet at the Grantley Adams International Airport. On the same day CEO, Robbie Burns, announced that the airline was itching to start selling tickets and get into the air, stating that the airline had already invested over 1 million USD into crew and staff hiring and training. Operations are scheduled to commence on May 8th 2011 with Trinidad being the first launched destination. Guyana and Jamaica will be launched on the 10th and 11th of May 2011 respectively.

Cargo

Both arrivals and departures terminals

Besides the Arrivals and Departures terminals, the Sir Grantley Adams International Airport also included provisions for a new cargo building in the 2000-2006 expansion project. The cargo needs of the airport include timely postal services in addition to various airline support. The cargo facility is located on the western end of the airport next to the new Arrivals building.
- Amerijet International
- Cargolux
- DHL Air
- FedEx Express
- Seawell Air Services (SAS) Limited
- Tampa Cargo
- United Parcel Service

Helicopter providers
- Bajan Helicopters - *Temporarily suspended*
- Horizon Helicopters

Other facilities

The head office of the Barbados Civil Aviation Department is located on the airport property, along the western edge of the arrivals terminal. In addition REDjet has its head office at the airport.
- On October 6, 1976, Cubana Flight 455 was bombed and crashed off the coast of Barbados in a terrorist attack by suspected CIA operatives shortly after the plane took off from Barbados. The plane had landed in Barbados, and was en route to another destination. Persons linked to the attack, and said to be hired by Luis Posada Carriles had de-planed in Barbados and made plans to fly out of the country a short time later on an alternate flight.
- In 2010, during the heightened traffic frequency of the tourist season (November through April), a number of chartered airlines and regularly scheduled carriers reported a series of 'bird strikes' on takeoff. These were not serious enough to cause any damage to the aircraft and they continued on to their destinations. After brief investigations, the 'birds' turned out to be small Vesper bats, native to Barbados.

Concorde Museum

Concorde 212 on display.

To the east of the main Sir Grantley Adams Airport is the 8534 m² site of the British Airways Concorde Museum on the old Spencers Plantation. The museum is part of the new expanded airport grounds. British Airways had granted the Government of Barbados one of their retired Concorde aircraft and BAC/SNIAS Concorde 212 G-BOAE is now on permanent display in a dedicated hall. The Q2 company had entered a museum and exhibition facility design to the Government of Barbados for this new permanent housing of the aircraft. The 'Concorde Experience' as a whole has a number of zones providing information on the aircraft.

On 2 November 1977 G-BOAE was the same aircraft that Queen Elizabeth II travelled flying from GAIA to London Heathrow, England. That occasion was the first visit by Concorde to Barbados.

"Alpha Echo" was also the last Concorde to fly supersonic on November 17, 2003, on its delivery flight to Barbados.

In popular culture

- Scenes of the airport are featured in season six of the television programme *Banged up Abroad*.
- TBPB is one of the featured airports in the aviation game Microsoft Flight Simulator X and Microsoft Flight Simulator 2004 & 2002.

Awards

- 2002, 2003, 2004 - The "Caribbean's Leading Airport" - by the World Travel Awards
- In 2010 Airport Council International (ACI) recognised the airport as one of the best facilities in the region for service excellence. Under the section Caribbean and Latin America, The Sir Grantley was ranked as third following: Guayaqui (GYE), Ecuador and Cancun (CUN), Mexico, respectively.

Source (edited): "http://en.wikipedia.org/wiki/Grantley_Adams_International_Airport"

List of airports in Barbados

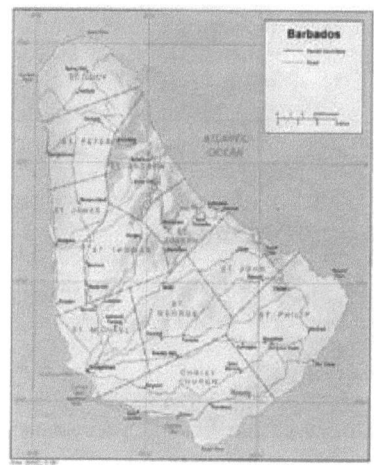

Map of Barbados

This is a **list of airports in Barbados**.

Barbados, situated just east of the Caribbean Sea, is a West Indian continental island-nation in the western Atlantic Ocean. It is considered a part of the Lesser Antilles. Its closest island neighbours are Martinique, Saint Lucia and Saint Vincent & the Grenadines to the west. To the south lies Trinidad and Tobago with which Barbados now shares a fixed official maritime boundary and also the South American mainland. Bridgetown is the capital and largest city in Barbados.

Airports

Airport names shown in **bold** indicate the airport has scheduled service on commercial airlines.

Source (edited): "http://en.wikipedia.org/wiki/List_of_airports_in_Barbados"

L.F. Wade International Airport

L.F. Wade International Airport (IATA: **BDA**, ICAO: **TXKF**), formerly named **Bermuda International Airport**, is the sole airport serving Bermuda, a British overseas territory in the North Atlantic Ocean. It is located in the parish of St. George's and is 10 miles (16 km) east of Bermuda's capital city of Hamilton. In 2006, L.F. Wade International Airport handled about 900,000 passengers, up 7% from 2005. It has one passenger terminal, one cargo terminal, eight aircraft stands and can support all aircraft sizes up to and including the Boeing 747. Currently, ten airlines operate seasonal or year-round scheduled services to Bermuda Airport from Canada, the United Kingdom, and the United States. The largest aircraft now operating in regularly scheduled service at BDA are British Airways' Boeing 777-200s.

History

The airfield began life as Kindley Field, a joint US Army Air Forces (USAAF)/Royal Air Force (RAF) base, during the Second World War. The RAF forces in Bermuda were withdrawn at the end of the War. The local RAF Commander, however, stayed on, on loan to the Bermuda Government, and converted the RAF facilities into the **Civil Air Terminal**, operated by the local government. When the pre-War airport, a flying boat facility on Darrell's Island, closed in 1948, Bermuda's air routes were taken over by land planes operating through the airfield, which by then was operated by the United States Air Force, as Kindley Air Force Base. In 1970, the field was transferred to the United States Navy, which operated it as US Naval Air Station, Bermuda until 1995 when the US Navy terminated its 99-year lease and the field was transferred to the Bermuda Government, which now operates the airport as part of the Ministry of Tourism & Transport.

The US Navy was not required to meet international civil air standards, despite the operation of civil airlines to the base. The Bermuda Government, however, was required to meet these standards very quickly on assuming control, and at some expense. This involved changes to the airfield lighting, erecting new fences, levelling anything over a certain height and within a certain distance of the runway (including the former base commander's residence, and the hill it stood on), and other changes.

The airport is located at the west of St. David's Island, and to the south of Ferry Reach. This places it in the *East End* of the archipelago, several miles from the current capital, Hamilton.

The airfield was constructed between 1941 and 1943 by levelling Longbird Island and several smaller islands, and filling in the waterways between them and St. David's Island. This created a landmass contiguous with St. David's, and the airfield is typically described as being in, or on, St. David's. The field originally had three runways, but only the longest is still in use. One of the others, most of which lies on a narrow peninsula, which juts into Castle Harbour, has been blocked by munitions bunkers that were built at the harbour end. There are further bunkers on the west side of the peninsula, and the US Navy had referred to the area as the *Weapons Pier*. Airport workers, today, refer to it as *The Finger*. The other former runway is used today as a taxiway to connect aprons one and two to the active runway, and the taxiway which parallels it. This was last used as a runway in 1978. It has its own former taxiway paralleling it, which now serves as a dispersal area for visiting aircraft.

On 16 April 2007, the airport was formally renamed "L.F. Wade International Airport" in honour of L. Frederick Wade, a past leader of the incumbent Governing party (the Progressive Labour Party) when it was in opposition. The name was criticised by the opposition United Bermuda Party for being politically biased.

Aerial view of Terminal

Current operations

In 2006, the airport handled almost one million passengers and had 258 airline flight arrivals and departures weekly during the peak June - August summer season. It has received high marks in passenger satisfaction surveys, placing first among North American airports in the "Under 15 million passengers" category in 2003 and fourth world-wide in its size category, according to the global airport monitor report that year. Cited were courtesy of staff, security, and check-in facilities.

The former NATO hangar built in the early 1990s is now used for the airport's growing corporate jet traffic. Because of Bermuda's considerable distance from the nearest land mass, the airport's use by General Aviation aircraft is limited to jets and long-range turboprops. Only jet fuel is available.

The airport offers U.S. Customs and Immigration preclearance, which means U.S.-bound passengers clear Customs in Bermuda; flights arriving in the U.S. from Bermuda are thus treated as domestic flights.

Air traffic control service is provided by BAS-Serco under contract to the DAO. The control tower is located on the north side of the airport (not to be confused with the old tower located at the terminal building) and provides service for most of the day and night. Approach, departure and enroute traffic control in the surrounding Oceanic Sector is provided by New York Air Route Traffic Control Center (ZNY), under an agreement between the U.S. Government's Federal Aviation Administration and the United Kingdom. The BDA tower controller and ZNY center controller are always in close contact. Remote radio transmitters and air traffic radar coverage at the airport also link Bermuda and New York Center.

A modern Doppler Weather Radar with a 150 mi. range was built by the DAO in 2005. Navaids at the airport, such as the Instrument Landing System (ILS) and VOR (VHF omnidirectional range), are owned by the DAO but maintained by BAS-Serco.

Terminal ramp

The airport is a United States government NASA Space Shuttle launch abort site. It can only be used during low and mid inclination launches.

The airport is also active in affairs of the Airports Council International, hosting the industry organisation's Legal Affairs Committee annual meeting in 2005. In 2006, Bermuda International Airport was selected as host for the Airport Council International's annual worldwide convention in 2010.

Airport agencies

- Department of Airport Operations (DAO) the airport operating authority - part of the Ministry of Tourism & Transport.
- Department of Civil Aviation (DCA) responsible for aircraft registration, safety regulation, and accident investigation - part of the Ministry of Tourism & Transport.
- Bermuda Immigration
- HM Customs
- US Customs and Border Protection, pre-clears passengers on most flights to USA.
- Airport Rescue Firefighting (ARFF), operated by Bermuda Fire Service from 2007
- Bermuda Fire Service, East-end station sits astride perimeter, and provides support to ARFF.
- Airport Security Police, enforces *airside* regulations and security under contract to the DAO.
- Bermuda Police Service, enforces *landside* parking and traffic regulations, and holds arrested persons.
- Bermuda Weather Service, operated by Serco under contract to the DAO.

Accidents and incidents

On 6 December 1952 A Cubana de Aviación DC-4 crashed after taking off from the airport killing 37 passengers out of 41 passengers and crew. See 1952 Bermuda air crash

Source (edited): "http://en.wikipedia.org/wiki/L.F._Wade_International_Airport"

List of airports in Bermuda

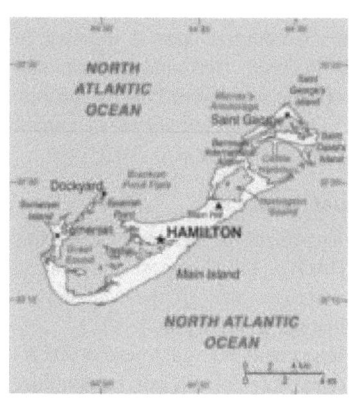

Map of Bermuda

This is a **list of airports in Bermuda**.

Bermuda, officially the Bermuda Islands, is a British overseas territory in the North Atlantic Ocean. Located off the east coast of the United States, its nearest landmass is Cape Hatteras, North Carolina, about 1,030 kilometres (640 mi) to the west-northwest. It is about 1,373 km (853 mi) south of Halifax, Nova Scotia, Canada, and 1,770 km (1,100 mi) northeast of Miami, Florida. The territory consists of approximately 138 islands, with a total area of 71.7 km² (27.7 sq. mi.). Its capital city is Hamilton.

Source (edited): "http://en.wikipedia.org/wiki/List_of_airports_in_Bermuda"

Abel Santamaría Airport

Abel Santamaría Airport (Spanish: *Aeropuerto "Abel Santamaría"*) (IATA: **SNU**, ICAO: **MUSC**) is an international airport serving Santa Clara, the capital city of the Villa Clara Province in Cuba.

Facilities

The airport resides at an elevation of 338 feet (103 m) above mean sea level. It has one runway designated 08/26 with an asphalt surface measuring 3,017 by 45 metres (9,898 × 148 ft).

The airport is also home to Mig-23BN fighters of the 14th Tactical Regiment of the Cuban Revolutionary Armed Forces, as well as helipads of military helicopters.

Santa Clara Air Base

The airport is an inactive Cuban Revolutionary Armed Forces air base:
- 14th Tactical Regiment - Mikoyan-Gurevich MiG-23 BN bombers and older Mikoyan-Gurevich MiG-23UB fighters
- Tactial Air Command - Mikoyan-Gurevich MiG-23 BN bombers and older Mikoyan-Gurevich MiG-23UB fighters
  - 2661st Bomber Squadron
- 1890th Interceptor Regiment - Mikoyan-Gurevich MiG-21B and UM fighters

Source (edited): "http://en.wikipedia.org/wiki/Abel_Santamar%C3%ADa_Airport"

Alberto Delgado Airport

Alberto Delgado Airport (Spanish: *Aeropuerto "Alberto Delgado"*) (IATA: **TND**, ICAO: **MUTD**) is an airport serving Trinidad, a city in the province of Sancti Spíritus in Cuba.

Facilities

The airport resides at an elevation of 125 feet (38 m) above mean sea level. It has one runway designated 06/24 with an asphalt surface measuring 1,801 by 30 metres (5,909 × 98 ft).

Source (edited): "http://en.wikipedia.org/wiki/Alberto_Delgado_Airport"

Antonio Maceo Airport

Antonio Maceo Airport (IATA: **SCU**, ICAO: **MUCU**) is an international airport located in Santiago, Cuba.

The airport has a drawing of *Che Guevara* on one of its outside walls. Pope John Paul II flew to this airport during his last visit to Cuba, flying round-trip between here and José Martí International Airport in Havana.

The airport is basically a turbo-prop center. Nevertheless, jets also fly to this airport. Most commercial flights into *SCU* are domestic, but there are about twenty international flights each week; while these international flights are done mostly by domestic airlines, the international routes have nevertheless awakened the interest of some foreign airlines that might open flights into this airport in the future.

Santiago de Cuba Base

The airport was home to the Cuban Revolutionary Armed Forces:

- 35th Transport Regiment - Antonov An-2 and Antonov An-26 transports
- 36th Helicopter Regiment - Mil Mi-8 and Mil Mi-24

The helipads are now part of the executive jet terminal on the north end of the airport.

Accidents and incidents

- On 4 November 2010, Aero Caribbean Flight 883, an ATR 72-212, crashed in the centre of the country with 68 people on board. The aircraft was flying from Santiago de Cuba to Havana when it went down. Twenty-eight foreigners were reported to be among the passengers. There were no survivors.

Source (edited): "http://en.wikipedia.org/wiki/Antonio_Maceo_Airport"

Carlos Manuel de Céspedes Airport

Carlos Manuel de Céspedes Airport (IATA: **BYM**, ICAO: **MUBY**) is a regional airport serving the city of Bayamo in the Granma Province of Cuba. It is named for Carlos Manuel de Céspedes.

Source (edited): "http://en.wikipedia.org/wiki/Carlos_Manuel_de_C%C3%A9spedes_Airport"

Cayo Coco Airport

Former runway of Cayo Coco airport, now highway

Cayo Coco (ICAO: **MUOC**) was an airport in Cayo Coco that served as the main airport of the island until it was superseded by the Jardines del Rey Airport, which opened in 2002. The former runway was incorporated as the new route of highway heading west connecting Cayo Coco with Cayo Guillermo, although some runway markings and taxiways remain visible. The airport terminal buildings and surrounding area have been reclaimed as a small natural park called Parque Natural El Baga.

Source (edited): "http://en.wikipedia.org/wiki/Cayo_Coco_Airport"

Ciudad Libertad Airport

Ciudad Libertad Airport (ICAO: **MULB**) is an airport serving Havana, Cuba. It was Cuba's main airport until 1930, when it was replaced by José Martí International Airport.

Facilities

The airport resides at an elevation of 98 feet (30 m) above mean sea level. It has one runway designated 08/26 with an asphalt surface measuring 2,065 by 50 metres (6,775 × 164 ft).

Source (edited): "http://en.wikipedia.org/wiki/Ciudad_Libertad_Airport"

ECASA

ECASA (Empresa Cubana de Aeropuertos y Servicios Aeronáuticos S.A.) is a government-owned company which operates 22 airports in Cuba, including José Martí International Airport, which serves Havana.

Other responsibilities of ECASA include air traffic control, aviation safety and baggage handling.

Source (edited): "http://en.wikipedia.org/wiki/ECASA"

Florida Airport (Cuba)

Florida Airport (ICAO: **MUFL**) is an airport serving Florida, a municipality in the province of Camagüey in Cuba.

Facilities

The airport resides at an elevation of

197 feet (60 m) above mean sea level. It has one runway designated 08/26 with an asphalt surface measuring 990 by 27 metres (3,248 × 89 ft).

Source (edited): "http://en.wikipedia.org/wiki/Florida_Airport_(Cuba)"

Frank País Airport

Frank País Airport (IATA: **HOG**, ICAO: **MUHG**) is an international airport that serves the city of Holguín in Cuba. It bears the name of Cuban revolutionary Frank País and is located in the municipio of Frank País.

Holguín Air Base

Airport interior

The airport is headquarters to the Cuban Revolutionary Armed Forces Eastern Command. The airport is also the base for two air regiments and fighter training centre:
- 1724th Interceptor Regiment
  - 3710th Interceptor Squadron and Training
  - 3840th Interceptor Squadron
  - 34th Tactical Regiment

The base is home to Mikoyan-Gurevich MiG-23BN ground attack bombers and Mikoyan-Gurevich MiG-21. The base is also home to a general purpose transport squadron using Mil Mi-17 (4-6) and stored at one end of the airport.

Source:
Source (edited): "http://en.wikipedia.org/wiki/Frank_Pa%C3%ADs_Airport"

Gustavo Rizo Airport

Gustavo Rizo Airport (IATA: **BCA**, ICAO: **MUBA**) is a regional airport that serves the town of Baracoa in Cuba. This is a small airport that usually operates with national flights. Located west of the bay near the Hotel Porto Santo and about 4 km (2½ miles) NNW of Baracoa. Although flights are infrequent, Cubana de Aviación flies here occasionally, from Santiago de Cuba, and the fare is very reasonable.

Airlines
- Cubana de Aviación (Havana)
- Aerocaribbean

Source (edited): "http://en.wikipedia.org/wiki/Gustavo_Rizo_Airport"

Hermanos Ameijeiras Airport

Hermanos Ameijeiras Airport (IATA: **VTU**, ICAO: **MUVT**) is a regional airport that serves the town of Las Tunas in Cuba.

Source (edited): "http://en.wikipedia.org/wiki/Hermanos_Ameijeiras_Airport"

Ignacio Agramonte International Airport

Ignacio Agramonte International Airport (IATA: **CMW**, ICAO: **MUCM**) is an international airport in the central province of Camaguey, Cuba. It serves the cities of Camaguey and Santa Lucia.

Note: All flights to the United States are operated as scheduled Special Authority Charters

World War II

During World War II, the airport was used by the United States Army Air Force Sixth Air Force from 1942 until 1944. The 25th Bombardment Group 417th Bombardment Squadron flew B-18 Bolo bombers from the airfield, known as **Camaguey Air Base**, from 13 April 1942 though August 1943. The squadron flew antisubmarine missions over the northern Caribbean. The base was also used for air-sea rescue missions by the 1st Rescue Squadron.

Camaguey Air Base

The airport is an inactive Cuban Revolutionary Armed Forces's (Camaguey) air base:
- 31st Regiment - third generation Mikoyan-Gurevich MiG-21MF jet fighter
- 3685th Regiment
  - 2 General purpose transport squadron - Mil Mi-17 helicopters

Source:
Source (edited): "http://en.wikipedia.org/wiki/Ignacio_Agramonte_International_Airport"

Jaime González Airport

Jaime González Airport (Spanish: *Aeropuerto "Jaime González"*) (IATA: **CFG**, ICAO: **MUCF**) is an international airport that serves Cienfuegos, a city on the southern coast of Cuba, and capital of the province of Cienfuegos.

Facilities

The airport resides at an elevation of 102 feet (31 m) above mean sea level. It has one runway designated 02/20 with an asphalt surface measuring 2,400 by 45 metres (7,874 × 148 ft).

Cienfuegos Air Base

The airport is an inactive Cuban Revolutionary Armed Forces air base:
- 15th Transport Regiment - Antonov An-2 and Antonov An-26 transport
- 16th Helicopter Regiment - Mil Mi-8, Mil Mi-14 and Mil Mi-17(Mi-8, Mi-14, Mi-17)
- 3684 Helicopter Regiment - Mil Mi-8TB transport helicopters, Mil Mi-24D attack/transport helicopter and Mil Mi-35 helicopter gunship/transport

Source:
Source (edited): "http://en.wikipedia.org/wiki/Jaime_Gonz%C3%A1lez_Airport"

Jardines del Rey Airport

Jardines del Rey Airport (IATA: **CCC**, ICAO: **MUCC**) is an airport situated on the Island of Cayo Coco, in the Ciego de Ávila Province, Cuba. The airport was inaugurated on December 26, 2002, replacing the earlier Cayo Coco Airport 10 km to the west. The airport is the only one in Cuba that has a shared administration with Aena, a Spanish company that manages 47 airports in Spain, twelve in Mexico and three in Colombia. Thousands of Canadian & European holiday makers pass through the airport every year. The airport serves holiday makers bound to both Cayo Guillermo and Cayo Coco.

Services

- VIP Lounges: The Airport has two VIP lounges, one belonging to Cubana de Aviación. The lounges provide tea/coffee, soft drinks, alcoholic drinks, snack bar, restaurant, TV, video, magazines/newspapers, check-in at class-differentiated counters, immigration and onboard control and flight information.
- Bank office: The airport has a bank office that is open 24 hours a day. This is the only office in the Keys that offers bank service on weekends.
- Shop: The airport has two duty free shops and one point of sale for books and music in the international departures area as well as a point of sale of drinks and cigars, in the check-in area.
- Snack bar and restaurant
- Nursery: At the disposal of the clients, there is a free service of nursery school, equipped with toys and attended by personnel of the airport.

Communications and access

By road: Access to the Jardines del Rey Airport is gained along a highway that links the tourist destination with the rest of the country. The island is united to the mainland by a 17 km (11 mi) causeway that starts from *Turiguanó* (to 40 km (25 mi) from the airport).

The times of access by highway are the following:
- Ciego de Avila: 75 min
- Morón: 50 min.
- Cayo Guillermo: 35 min.
- Cayo Coco: 15 min.

There is no regular bus route that links the mentioned cities to the airport.
Source (edited): "http://en.wikipedia.org/wiki/Jardines_del_Rey_Airport"

Joaquín de Agüero Airport

Joaquín de Agüero Airport (Spanish: *Aeropuerto "Joaquín de Agüero"*) (ICAO: **MUSL**), also known as **Santa Lucia Airport**, is an airport serving Playa Santa Lucia, in the Camagüey Province in Cuba.

Facilities

The airport resides at an elevation of 13 feet (4 m) above mean sea level. It has one runway designated 07/25 with an asphalt surface measuring 1,800 by 30 metres (5,906 × 98 ft).

Source (edited): "http://en.wikipedia.org/wiki/Joaqu%C3%ADn_de_Ag%C3%BCero_Airport"

José Martí International Airport

José Martí International Airport (IATA: **HAV**, ICAO: **MUHA**), previously called **El Rancho Boyeros International Airport**, is located 15 km (9 mi) southwest of Havana, Cuba, and is a hub for Cubana de Aviación, Aerogaviota and Aero Caribbean, and former Latin American hub for Aeroflot Soviet Airlines. The airport lies in the municipality of Boyeros. It is named in memory of patriot and poet José Martí.

Havana airport is operated by *ECASA* (Empresa Cubana de Aeropuertos y Servicios Aeronáuticos S.A.). It is Cuba's main international and domestic gateway, it serves several million passengers each year, 80% of Cuba's international passengers along with Varadero's Juan Gualberto Gómez Airport.

There are currently three terminals in use at the airport plus an additional terminal operated only by Aero Caribbean.

History

The construction of José Martí Airport was authorized in March 1929. On 24 February 1930, the airport officially opened, replacing *Havana Columbia Airport*. On 30 October 1930, Cubana de Aviación's (at the time CNCAC, S.A.) first ever flight Havana-Santiago de Cuba carried the mail using a Ford trimotor with stops in Santa Clara, Morón and Camaguey. In 1936 non-commercial flights to Madrid started with an Lockheed Sirius aircraft made out of wood lined with cloth, had a Pratt & Whitney Wasp 550 hp (410 kW) engine, a cruising speed of 180 mph and no radio. The aircraft named "4th of September" was commanded by Capt. Antonio Menéndez Pélaez and was flown previously between Camaguey, Cuba and Seville, Spain. By January 1943 the airport had its first control tower and was as well the first control tower in the country. The first commercial international flight out of the airport was flown by Cubana de Aviación's DC-3 Havana-Miami. By 1950 the airport had a second route to Europe, the flight known as "The route of the stars" Havana-Rome operated by a Cubana DC-4.

In 1961 the relations with the United States deteriorated substantially and with the United States embargo against Cuba, airlines from the United States were not permitted to operate regularly scheduled flights to the airport. In the 1990s special charter flights were approved by the US government to operate from Miami to José Martí for Cuban citizens living in the United States that have close relatives in Cuba. Today, various airlines operate non-stop service between Havana and Miami, including American Eagle Airlines, Gulfstream International Airlines, and several others.

Because of Cuba's relationship with the Soviet Union, the airport during the 1970s and 1980s enjoyed the presence of many Eastern Bloc airline companies, Aeroflot, Czech Airlines, Interflug, LOT. The airport has seen its share of tragedies, as many of the older Soviet built jets that Cubana and some of the other communist airlines (such as the Soviet Union's Aeroflot and the East German Interflug) used have crashed either going from or to this airport.

Terminal 2 opened on 15 November 1988 primarily for direct flights to the United States and charter flights. Ten years later on 27 April 1998, the new international terminal 3 was opened by Canada's Prime Minister Jean Chrétien and Cuban President Fidel Castro. The new terminal with three VIP lounges provides many modern facilities and jetways that the former international terminal 1 did not provide.

In 2002, the Air Freight Logistics Enterprise (ELCA S.A.) opened José Martí's first freight terminal, the freight terminal is a joint venture equally shared between the Cargosur company, part of the Iberia group, and Aerovaradero S.A. of Cuba, with an investment of over $2.5 million USD. The goal of this enterprise, the most modern of its kind in this geographical region, is to facilitate and reduce the cost of freight transportation between Europe and the Americas, in aircraft belonging to various companies. The terminal has a 600-Ton capacity, 2,000 cubic meters of space in two refrigeration and freezing chambers alone, with humidity and gas controls.

Domestic Terminal 1

Aeroflot aircraft at Terminal 3

Air France aircraft at gate 11

T3 departure gates

The airport is home to IBECA. As part of Cubana's renovation strategy, the airline has sought to upgrade its technical support capabilities, and in 2005 IBECA was created. IBECA is a joint venture company 50% owned by Cubana de Aviación and 50% by Iberia

Airlines, it deals with the technical maintenance of Western-built aircraft, including all Airbus and Boeing models. It has contracted with various airlines flying to Cuba to provide maintenance and technical support. Annually, it gives technical coverage to more than 5,000 air operations, for more than 30 different airlines, primarity from Europe and the Americas.

Presently José Martí Airport is constructing a new automated center of air traffic control which will give its service to the whole region of the FIR assigned to Cuba. The total radarization of FIR was a prior necessary step, this will completely increase the reliability of the air traffic service that Cuba has in the whole region under its control, which is one the major air traffic volume of Latin America as most flights to/from the east coast United States to Central and South America fly over Cuba's air space, with an estimated over 450 controlled flights daily.

Facilities

Terminals

Terminal 1 used to be the main international and domestic terminal building in the airport prior of the opening of terminal 2, and 3-which was constructed in 1998. The terminal is located on the west side of runway 6. It is now used primarily for domestic flights.

Terminal 2 handles mainly schedule charter flights to and from Miami and New York for US residents with special permission from the United States government and Cuban citizens with US visas, the scheduled charters are operated by Gulfstream Air Charters, ABC Charters, Marazul Charters and C & T Charters. The terminal is located on the north side, just in front of runway 24 threshold. It was constructed in the 1988 when the first charter flights after the revolution were opened from Miami. There are bars, bookshops, newsagents, and also a restaurant on the second floor, as well as car rentals in the arrivals area.

Terminal 3 is the main international terminal, it was open in 1998 by Canada's Prime Minister Jean Chrétien and Fidel Castro, and is the largest and most modern. Ticketing and departures are located on the upper level, arrivals and baggage carousels are located on the lower level. There are several car rentals located in the Arrivals Area, the companies represented include Cubanacar, Fenix, Rent a Car, Rex (limousines and luxury cars), Transtur, and Via Rent-a-Car. In terminal 3 all the bars and restaurants are open 24 hours. There are information desks in the Arrivals and Departure areas. A bank, post office and internet are also available in this terminal.

Terminal 5 is mainly used by Aerocaribbean, but Aerotaxi, which is a Cuban based charter airline, is also present. All flights from the United States will temporarily be handled at this terminal due to construction and remodeling at Terminal 2.

Transfer Between Terminals

There is a bus service between the terminals.

Parking

The airport has short-term car parks. Terminal 3 has 750 parking spaces and Terminal 1 & 2 has 500 parking spaces each. All car parks are situated less than 150 meters from the terminals.

Note

- **Note 1:** All flights to the United States are operated as scheduled Special Authority Charters

Accidents and incidents

- "1977 Aeroflot Ilyushin 62 crash" on 27 May killed 68 of the 70 on-board and one person on the ground. At the time the accident was the deadliest aviation accident in Cuba's history. It remains the second deadliest in Cuba's history. One of the victims was José Carlos Schwarz, a poet and musician from Guinea-Bissau.
- On 3 September 1989, a Cubana de Aviación Ilyushin 62M (CU-T1281) on a non-scheduled international passenger flight to Cologne (Cologne Bonn Airport), Germany crashed shortly after take-off. All of the 115 passengers and 11 crew members as well as 45 persons on the ground were killed and the aircraft was written off. One of the persons on board was Roberto Volponi, son of the writer Paolo Volponi.
- On 31 March 2003, a Blue Panorama Airlines Boeing 767 (EI-CXO) skidded off the main runway 06 in poor weather and gusting winds. No injuries occurred.
- On 3 May 2007, two army recruits hijacked a plane destined for Miami at José Martí International Airport in Havana. The men killed a hostage before being arrested prior to takeoff. It was the first Cuban hijacking attempt reported since the spring of 2003.
- On 4 November 2010, Aero Caribbean Flight 883, an ATR 72-212, crashed in the centre of the country with 68 people on board. The aircraft was flying from Santiago de Cuba to Havana when it went down. Twenty-eight foreigners were reported to be among the passengers. There were no survivors.

Source (edited): "http://en.wikipedia.org/wiki/Jos%C3%A9_Mart%C3%AD_International_Airport"

Juan Gualberto Gómez Airport

Juan Gualberto Gómez Airport (IATA: **VRA**, ICAO: **MUVR**) is an international airport serving Varadero, Cuba and the province of Matanzas. The airport is located closer to the town of Matanzas than to Varadero. The closest airport to Varadero is Santa Marta Airport. Juan Gualberto Gómez Airport is the second busiest airport in Cuba after José Martí International Airport in Havana.

The terminal building has a few

shops, duty free shop, cafeterias and crowded lounges. The ground handling equipment is imported mainly from North America.

There are three jet bridges, but air stairs are used for the remaining aircraft parking spaces on the apron by the terminal.

The airport is named for journalist and black rights activist in Cuba Juan Gualberto Gómez (1854-1933).

Air Canada Airbus A321 departing Varadero Airport

Departures hall

Incidents

There has been 5 significant incidents involving aircraft from or enroute to the airport since the 1950s. Only 1 flight involved resulted in fatalities. Three flights involved Cubans hijacking an aircraft to flee to the United States.

- March 6, 2005 - Air Transat Flight 961 Airbus A310 returned safely to airport following detachment of rudder after take off.
- December 29, 1992 - Aerocaribbean Antonov 26 was hijacked enroute to Varadero Airport from Havana. Aircraft lands in Miami.
- July 3, 1961 - Cubana de Aviación Douglas DC-3 was hijacked enroute to Varadero Airport from Havana. Aircraft lands in Miami.
- April 25, 1959 - Cubana de Aviación Vickers Viscount was hijacked after takeoff from Juan Gualberto Gómez Airport and forced to land at Key West International Airport.
- November 1, 1958 - Cubana de Aviación Flight 495 Vickers Viscount 755D crashes in Nipe Bay when attempting an emergency landing at Preston Airport. Plane was enroute to Varadero from Miami with 20 onboard. Only 3 survived with 17 fatalities.

Source (edited): "http://en.wikipedia.org/wiki/Juan_Gualberto_G%C3%B3mez_Airport"

Kawama Airport

Kawama Airport (Spanish: *Aeropuerto "Kawama"*) (ICAO: **MUKW**) is an airport serving Kawama, in the Matanzas Province in Cuba.

Facilities

The airport resides at an elevation of 16 feet (5 m) above mean sea level. It has one runway designated 06/24 with an asphalt surface measuring 1,300 by 45 metres (4,265 × 148 ft).

Source (edited): "http://en.wikipedia.org/wiki/Kawama_Airport"

La Coloma Airport

La Coloma Airport (Spanish: *Aeropuerto "La Coloma"*) (IATA: **LCL**, ICAO: **MULM**) is an airport serving La Coloma, in the Pinar del Río Province in Cuba.

Facilities

The airport resides at an elevation of 131 feet (40 m) above mean sea level. It has one runway designated 07/25 with an asphalt surface measuring 1,992 by 45 metres (6,535 × 148 ft).

La Coloma Air Training

The airport is home to a training unit of the Cuban Revolutionary Armed Forces:

- 1660th Primary Training Squadron (L-39C)

Source:
Source (edited): "http://en.wikipedia.org/wiki/La_Coloma_Airport"

Las Brujas Airport (Cuba)

Las Brujas Airport (ICAO: **MUBR**) is an airport serving Cayo Santa Maria, in the Villa Clara Province in Cuba.

Facilities

The airport resides at an elevation of 13 feet (4 m) above mean sea level. It has one runway designated 09/27 with an asphalt surface measuring 1,803 by 44 metres (5,915 × 144 ft).

Source (edited): "http://en.wikipedia.org/wiki/Las_Brujas_Airport_(Cuba)"

Leeward Point Field

Leeward Point Field (IATA: **NBW**, ICAO: **MUGM**), also known as **Leeward Airfield**, is a U.S. military airfield located at Naval Station Guantanamo Bay in Guantánamo Bay, Cuba.

Facilities

The airport resides at an elevation of 56 feet (17 m) above mean sea level. It has one runway designated 10/28 with an asphalt surface measuring 2,438 by 61 metres (7,999 × 200 ft).
Source (edited): "http://en.wikipedia.org/wiki/Leeward_Point_Field"

List of airports in Cuba

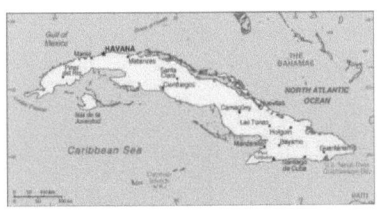

Map of Cuba

This is a **list of airports in Cuba**, grouped by type and sorted by location.

Cuba, officially the Republic of Cuba, is an island country in the Caribbean. It is an archipelago of islands located in the northern Caribbean Sea at the confluence with the Gulf of Mexico and the Atlantic Ocean. The United States lies to the northwest, the Bahamas to the north, Haiti to the east, Jamaica and the Cayman Islands to the south, and Mexico to the west. The country is subdivided into 14 provinces and one special municipality (Isla de la Juventud, the country's second largest island). Cuba's capital and largest city is Havana.

Airports

Airport names shown in **bold** have scheduled passenger service on commercial airlines.
Source (edited): "http://en.wikipedia.org/wiki/List_of_airports_in_Cuba"

Mariana Grajales Airport

Mariana Grajales Airport (IATA: **GAO**, ICAO: **MUGT**) is an airport serving Guantánamo, a city in Cuba.

Facilities

The airport resides at an elevation of 56 feet (17 m) above mean sea level. It has one runway designated 17/35 with an asphalt surface measuring 2,358 by 46 metres (7,736 × 151 ft).
Source (edited): "http://en.wikipedia.org/wiki/Mariana_Grajales_Airport"

Máximo Gómez Airport

Máximo Gómez Airport (IATA: **AVI**, ICAO: **MUCA**) is a regional airport in the Ciego de Ávila Province of Cuba which serves the city of Ciego de Ávila.

It is named for Máximo Gómez, a Major General in the Ten Years' War (1868–1878) and Cuba's military commander in the Cuban War of Independence (1895–1898).

Source (edited): "http://en.wikipedia.org/wiki/M%C3%A1ximo_G%C3%B3mez_Airport"

Nicaro Airport

Nicaro Airport (IATA: **ICR**, ICAO: **MUNC**) is an airfield serving Nicaro in Cuba.

Facilities

The airport resides at an elevation of 26 feet (8 m) above mean sea level. It has one runway which measures 1,800 metres (5,906 ft) in length.

Former Airbase

The airfield was once used by the Cuban Revolutionary Armed Forces, but no military aircraft or buildings exists on the site.
The abandoned airfield once had a single 4314 ft runway.
Source (edited): "http://en.wikipedia.org/wiki/Nicaro_Airport"

Orestes Acosta Airport

Orestes Acosta Airport (Spanish: *Aeropuerto Orestes Acosta*) (IATA: **MOA**, ICAO: **MUMO**) is a regional

Pinar del Río Airport

Pinar del Río Airport (IATA: **QPD**, ICAO: **MUPR**) is an airport serving Pinar del Río, the capital city of the Pinar del Río Province in Cuba.

Facilities
The airport resides at an elevation of 131 feet (40 m) above mean sea level. It has one runway designated 08/26 with an asphalt surface measuring 1,120 by 37 metres (3,675 × 121 ft).
Source (edited): "http://en.wikipedia.org/wiki/Pinar_del_R%C3%ADo_Airport"

Playa Baracoa Airport

Playa Baracoa Airport (IATA: **UPB**, ICAO: **MUPB**) is a regional airport west of Havana, Cuba that serves regional flights in Cuba.

Airlines
- Cubana de Aviación (Varadero)
- Aerogaviota (Cayo Largo)

Playa Baracoa Air Base
The airport is an inactive Cuban Revolutionary Armed Forces air base and home to Air Defense Command and VIP transport:
- - 3710th Interceptor Squadron and Training
- 3688 Transport Regiment - using Antonov An-26 transport
  - 3405 Executive Transport Squadron - Yakovlev Yak-40 VIP jet, Antonov An-26M transport; Mil Mi-8P and Mil Mi-8TB transport helicopters
- 3404 Transport Squadron - using Antonov An-2 transport

Source:
Source (edited): "http://en.wikipedia.org/wiki/Playa_Baracoa_Airport"

Rafael Cabrera Airport

Rafael Cabrera Airport or **Rafael Cabrera Mustelier Airport** (Spanish: *Aeropuerto "Rafael Cabrera"*) (IATA: **GER**, ICAO: **MUNG**) is an airport serving Nueva Gerona, the capital city of the Isla de la Juventud special municipality in Cuba.

Facilities
The airport resides at an elevation of 79 feet (24 m) above mean sea level. It has two asphalt paved runways: 05/23 is 2,500 by 45 metres (8,202 × 148 ft) and 17/35 is 1,623 by 30 metres (5,325 × 98 ft).

Airlines and destinations
The only airline to use the airport is Cuban flag carrier Cubana de Aviación, which operates flights to and from Havana, Toronto, and Mexico City.
Source (edited): "http://en.wikipedia.org/wiki/Rafael_Cabrera_Airport"

Rafael Pérez Airport

Gustavo Rizo Airport (IATA: **GER**, ICAO: **MUNG**) is a regional airport that serves the town of Nueva Gerona in Cuba.

Airlines
- Cubana de Aviación (Havana)

Source (edited): "http://en.wikipedia.org/wiki/Rafael_P%C3%A9rez_Airport"

San Antonio de los Baños Air Base

San Antonio de los Baños Air Base (ICAO: **MUSA**) is a military air base located near San Antonio de los Baños, a municipality in the province of Havana (La Habana) in Cuba.

During the Cuban Missile Crisis, Soviet Armed Forces elements deployed as part of Operation Anadyr were based at the airfield. the 32nd Guards Fighter Aviation Regiment of the Soviet Air Forces, flying MiG-21F-13s, had elements here. Initially the regiment sent its 2nd Squadron from Santa Clara air base to San Antonio de los Banos, and then later the whole regiment was concentrated at San Antonio de los Banos. In 1963 the regiment transferred its aircraft to the Cuban Air Force and returned home. In Cuba the regiment served under the title 213th Fighter Aviation Regiment.

Facilities

The air base resides at an elevation of 164 feet (50 m) above mean sea level. It has three concrete paved runways: Runway 05/23 is 3,596 by 56 metres (11,798 × 184 ft), Runway 12/30 is 2,482 by 46 metres (8,143 × 151 ft), and Runway 01/19 is 2,400 by 46 metres (7,874 × 151 ft).

San Antonio de los Banos Air Base

The airport is an inactive Cuban Revolutionary Armed Forces airbase:
- 21st Regiment - Mikoyan-Gurevich MiG-21 fighter
- 1724th Regiment
- 1779th Regiment - Mikoyan MiG-29A and UB, Mikoyan-Gurevich MiG-23ML and UB fighters
- 4768 Intercept Squadron - Mikoyan-Gurevich MiG-211B bombers and Mikoyan-Gurevich MiG-21UM fighters

Source (edited): "http://en.wikipedia.org/wiki/San_Antonio_de_los_Ba%C3%B1os_Air_Base"

San Nicolás de Bari Airport

San Nicolás de Bari Airport (ICAO: **MUNB**) is an airport serving San Nicolás de Bari, a municipality of the Havana (La Habana) province in Cuba.

Facilities

The airport resides at an elevation of 49 feet (15 m) above mean sea level. It has one runway designated 06/24 with an asphalt surface measuring 1,023 by 24 metres (3,356 × 79 ft).

Source (edited): "http://en.wikipedia.org/wiki/San_Nicol%C3%A1s_de_Bari_Airport"

Sancti Spíritus Airport

Sancti Spíritus Airport (IATA: **USS**, ICAO: **MUSS**) is an airport serving Sancti Spíritus, the capital city of the Sancti Spíritus Province in Cuba.

Facilities

The airport resides at an elevation of 295 feet (90 m) above mean sea level. It has one runway designated 03/21 with an asphalt surface measuring 1,801 by 29 metres (5,909 × 95 ft).

Sancti Spirtus Air Base

The airport is an inactive Cuban Revolutionary Armed Forces air base:
- 12th Regiment - Mikoyan-Gurevich MiG-24MF fighters

Source (edited): "http://en.wikipedia.org/wiki/Sancti_Sp%C3%ADritus_Airport"

Sierra Maestra Airport

Sierra Maestra Airport (IATA: **MZO**, ICAO: **MUMZ**) is a regional airport that serves the town of Manzanillo in Cuba.

Source (edited): "http://en.wikipedia.org/wiki/Sierra_Maestra_Airport"

Siguanea Airport

Siguanea Airport (Spanish: *Aeropuerto "Siguanea"*) (IATA: **SZJ**, ICAO: **MUSN**) is an airport serving Siguanea, in the Isla de la Juventud special municipality in Cuba.

Facilities

The airport resides at an elevation of 39 feet (12 m) above mean sea level. It has one runway designated 05/23 with an asphalt surface measuring 1,800 by 30 metres (5,906 × 98 ft).

Source (edited): "http://en.wikipedia.org/wiki/Siguanea_Airport"

Vilo Acuña Airport

Vilo Acuña Airport or **Juan Vitalio Acuña Airport** (Spanish: *Aeropuerto "Vitalio Acuña"*) (IATA: **CYO**, ICAO: **MUCL**) is an international airport serving Cayo Largo del Sur, a small coral island in Cuba. It is located within the special municipality (*municipio especial*) of Isla de la Juventud.

Facilities

The airport resides at an elevation of 10 feet (3 m) above mean sea level. It has one runway designated 12/30 with an asphalt surface measuring 3,008 by 45 metres (9,869 × 148 ft).

Source (edited): "http://en.wikipedia.org/wiki/Vilo_Acu%C3%B1a_Airport"

Hato International Airport

Hato International Airport or **Curaçao International Airport** (originally named *Dr. Albert Plesman International Airport*) (IATA: **CUR**, ICAO: **TNCC**) is the airport of Willemstad, Curaçao. It has services to the Caribbean region, South America, North America and Europe. Hato Airport is a fairly large facility, with the third longest commercial runway in the Caribbean region (after Rafael Hernández Airport and Pointe-à-Pitre International Airport). The airport was the hub of Air ALM and its successor Dutch Caribbean Airlines, the flag carriers of the former Netherlands Antilles until the latter ceased operations in 2004. The airport is now the home base of Dutch Antilles Express and Insel Air.

A new terminal was officially opened in 2006 and it accommodates a maximum of 1.6 million passengers per year.

The New Curaçao terminal at dusk.

World War II

During World War II, the airport was used by the United States Army Air Force Sixth Air Force conducting antisubmarine patrols. Flying units using the airfield were:

- 59th Bombardment Squadron (VI Bomber Command) 10 March 1942-13 July 1943 (A-20 Havoc)
- 32d Fighter Squadron (36th Fighter Group, Antilles Air Command, XXVI Fighter Command) 9 March 1943-13 March 1944, (P-40 Warhawk)

Detachment operated from: Dakota Field, Aruba, 9 March 1943-9 March 1944

Detachment operated from: Losey Army Airfield, Puerto Rico, 9 March-4 June 1944

- 25th Bombardment Group (VI Bomber Command), 1 August-5 October 1943

Coastguard Air Station HATO

Located at the west side of Hato Airport there is a small hangar for the 2 Dash-8 patrol aircraft of the Coast Guard Netherlands Antilles & Aruba. This was until 2007 a naval airbase of the Royal Netherlands Navy who operated the base for 55 years. With a wide variety of aircraft in the past years Fireflies, Avengers, Trackers, Neptunes, Fokker F-27's, PC-3 Orions, Fokker F-60's and several helicopters. After the political decision to sell all Orions the airbase wasn't needed anymore.

And west of the air station the US Air force operate a Forward Operating Base (FOB) mostly operate AWAC's and transport aircraft. Until 1999 the US Air force operated a small amount of F-16's from the FOB.

Source (edited): "http://en.wikipedia.org/wiki/Hato_International_Airport"

List of airports in Guadeloupe

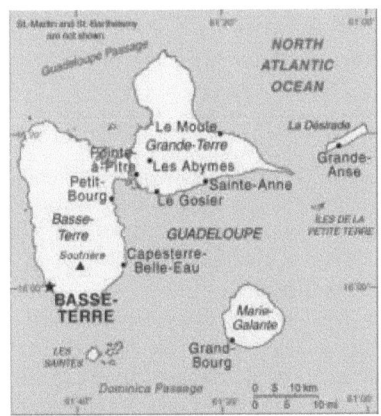

Map showing the islands of Guadeloupe.

This is a **list of airports in Guadeloupe**, sorted by location.

Guadeloupe is an archipelago located in the eastern Caribbean Sea. It is an overseas department (French: *département d'outre-mer* or *DOM*) of France. Guadeloupe comprises five islands: Basse-Terre Island, Grande-Terre (separated from Basse-Terre by a narrow sea channel called Salt River) with the adjacent islands of La Désirade, Les Saintes and Marie-Galante.

Further to the north, Saint-Barthélemy and the French part of Saint Martin once came under the jurisdiction of Guadeloupe, but each is now an overseas collectivity (*collectivités d'outremer* or *COM*) of France.

Airports

ICAO location identifiers are linked to each airport's Aeronautical Information Publication (AIP), which are available online in Portable Document Format (PDF) from the French *Service d'information aéronautique* (SIA).

Source (edited): "http://en.wikipedia.org/wiki/List_of_airports_in_Guadeloupe"

Marie-Galante Airport

Marie-Galante Airport (IATA: **GBJ**, ICAO: **TFFM**) is an airport serving the island of Marie-Galante in Guadeloupe. It is located 5.5 km (3.0 NM) east of Grand-Bourg, one of three communes on the island.

Facilities

The airport resides at an elevation of 17 feet (5 m) above mean sea level. It has one paved runway designated 09/27 which measures 1,240 by 30 metres (4,068 × 98 ft).

Source (edited): "http://en.wikipedia.org/wiki/Marie-Galante_Airport"

Pointe-à-Pitre International Airport

Pointe-à-Pitre International Airport or **Pointe-à-Pitre Le Raizet Airport** (French: *Aérodrome de Pointe-à-Pitre Le Raizet* or *Aéroport Guadeloupe Pôle Caraïbes* "Caribbean Hub") (IATA: **PTP**, ICAO: **TFFR**) is an airport serving Pointe-à-Pitre on the island of Grande-Terre in Guadeloupe. The airport is located in Abymes, 2.4 km (1.3 NM) north-northeast of Pointe-à-Pitre. It is the main hub for Air Caraïbes and Air Antilles Express. It is the largest of the six airports in the archipelago. In 2008, the airport handled between 2 and 2.5 million passengers, it is the second busiest airport in the Lesser Antilles after Grantley Adams International Airport.

Facilities

The airport resides at an elevation of 35 feet (11 m) above mean sea level. It has one paved runway designated 11/29 which measures 3,125 by 45 metres (10,253 × 148 ft).

Runway 11/29 is long enough allowing aircraft as large as the A380 to take off and land without difficulty. The airport was also one of the first to handle the first A380 prototype in the 2nd week of January 2006, for 2 days. The same year, the airport celebrated its 40th anniversary.

At one time, Air Guadeloupe had its head office on the airport property.

Source (edited): "http://en.wikipedia.org/wiki/Pointe-%C3%A0-Pitre_International_Airport"

List of airports in Martinique

A **list of airports in Martinique**, sorted by location.

Martinique is an island in the eastern Caribbean Sea. It is an overseas department (French: *département d'outre-mer*, *DOM*) of France.

ICAO location identifiers are linked to each airport's Aeronautical Information Publication (AIP), which are available online in Portable Document Format (PDF) from the French *Service d'information aéronautique* (SIA). Locations shown in bold are as per the airport's AIP page.

Source (edited): "http://en.wikipedia.org/wiki/List_of_airports_in_Martinique"

Martinique Aimé Césaire International Airport

Martinique Aimé Césaire International Airport (French: *Aéroport International Martinique Aimé Césaire*) (IATA: **FDF**, ICAO: **TFFF**) is the international airport of Martinique in the French West Indies. Located in Le Lamentin, a suburb of the capital Fort-de-France, it was opened in 1950 and renamed in 2007 after author and politician Aimé Césaire.

Air taxi
- ATIS (Air Tourisme Instruction Services)
- ATIS or AIRAWAK

Tour operators
- Afat Voyages
- Alizes Voyages
- Carre d'As
- SMCR Voyages
- Laroc Voyages
- Look Voyages
- Nouvelles Frontieres
- Selectour
- Yssa Voyages

Facilities
The airport resides at an elevation of 16 feet (5 m) above mean sea level. It has one runway designated 09/27 with an asphalt surface measuring 3,300 by 45 metres (10,827 × 148 ft).

Passenger facilities
Police, customs, bagage claim, pharmacy, bagage claim, vaccination bureau, handicap facilities, tobacconist, bank, money changing, souvenir shops, tax-free shopping, gift shop, florist, hairdresser, car rentals, taxi, parking, restaurants, cafés and bars, two hotels (Hôtel La Galléria and Hôtel Valmenière)

Other facilities
When Air Martinique existed, its head office was on the airport property.

Fixed base operators, fuels and repairs
Trans services Antilles, Martinique Ground Handing, Aircraft Global Assistant, Jet Aviation Services, GPAF, SOCAMA, Air Techs, Atis

Cargo facilities
1x 747 Freighter Dock, Bonded Warehouse, Transit Zone, Mechanical Handling, Heated Storage, Refrigerated Storage, Mortuary, Fresh Meat Inspection, Health Officials, Very Large/Heavy Cargo, Express/Courier Centre Source (edited): "http://en.wikipedia.org/wiki/Martinique_Aim%C3%A9_C%C3%A9saire_International_Airport"

Juancho E. Yrausquin Airport

The runway at Juancho E. Irausquin Airport.

The airport building.

Juancho E. Irausquin Airport (IATA: **SAB**, ICAO: **TNCS**) is the only airport on the Caribbean island of Saba. It is well known among professional pilots for the way in which airplanes must approach or take off from the airport.

Information
Despite a reputation as the most dangerous airport in the world, no accidents have occurred at Juancho E. Irausquin. The airport's risky reputation arises from the airport's physical position: it is flanked on one side by high hills; and on the runway's other side and both ends, cliffs drop into the sea. Additionally, the runway at the airport is extremely short (400m); this creates the possibility that an airplane could under/overshoot the runway during landing or takeoff and end up in the sea or dashed on the rocky cliffs.

Although the airport is officially marked as closed to traffic, regional airline propeller aircraft are able to land there under waivers from The Netherlands Antilles' Civil Aviation Authority. The most common aircraft to land there are the Twin Otter and BN-2 Islander

Irausquin Airport can be seen from some places in Saint Martin.

Facilities

Jet aircraft are unable to land at the airport, because the runway is too short (approx. 1,300 ft or 396 m). However, smaller airplanes (DHC-6, BN-2 and helicopters) are common sights there. There is a small ramp and terminal on the south side of the runway. The ramp also has a designated helipad. The terminal building houses offices for Winair, immigration and security, a fire department with one fire truck and a tower. The tower is an advisory service only and does not provide air traffic control. Aviation fuel is not available on the island of Saba.

The only airline currently serving Irausquin Airport is locally owned Winair, which operates daily flights to Sint Maarten and Sint Eustatius aboard a de Havilland Canada DHC-6 Twin Otter. The flight to Sint Maarten takes about twelve minutes.

Source (edited): "http://en.wikipedia.org/wiki/Juancho_E._Yrausquin_Airport"

Gustaf III Airport

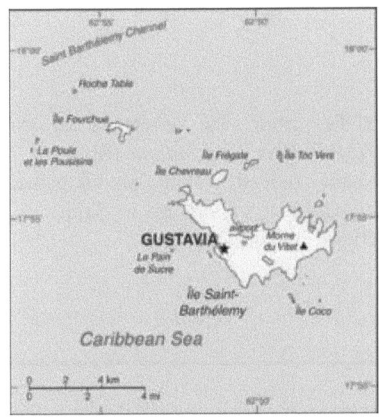

Map of Saint Barthélemy with location of airport.

Gustaf III Airport (IATA: **SBH**, ICAO: **TFFJ**), also known as **Saint Barthélemy Airport** or **St. Jean Airport** (French: *Aérodrome de St Jean*), is a public use airport located in the village of St. Jean on the Caribbean island of Saint Barthélemy. Both the airport and the island's main town of Gustavia are named for King Gustav III of Sweden, under whom Sweden obtained the island from France in 1785 (it was sold back to France in 1878).

In 1984, swedish Minister of Communications, Hans Gustafsson, inaugurated the terminal building of the Gustaf III Airport.

The local Saint-Barths check the comings and goings of the island from 8:00 in the morning till darkness at 18:00, when the airport closes.

The Saint-Barths are divided on the issue of lighting at the airport for emergency purposes. There is a risk then that the traffic to the island would increase, but more importantly there is the issue of night-time noise disruption.

The airport is served by small regional commercial aircraft and charters. Most visiting aircraft carry fewer than twenty passengers, such as the Twin Otter, a common sight around Saint Barth and throughout the northern West Indies. The short airstrip is at the base of a gentle slope ending directly on the beach. The arrival descent is extremely steep over the hilltop traffic circle and departing planes fly right over the heads of sunbathers (although small signs advise sunbathers not to lie directly at the end of the runway). The airport is located in the island's second-largest town, St. Jean.

The History Channel program *Most Extreme Airports*, ranks Gustaf III airport, which is casually referred to as "St. Barth's", as the 3rd most dangerous airport in the world.

Incidents and accidents

A Piper PA-23 Aztec attempted the tricky Runway 10 landing on May 23, 2009, eventually touching down 700 feet from the departure end of the runway. Amateur video of the crash sequence shows the plane approaching higher and faster than usual before making the dive for the runway. The plane gained more speed on descent and was caught in ground effect; resultingly, the pilot fought the plane onto the runway, then locked its brakes to stop. Instead, the plane continued into sand, its nosegear dug in and nearly flipped over. Nobody aboard was injured.

Source (edited): "http://en.wikipedia.org/wiki/Gustaf_III_Airport"

List of airports in Saint Barthélemy

A **list of airports in Saint Barthélemy**, sorted by location.

Saint Barthélemy (French: *Saint-Barthélemy*) is an island in the eastern Caribbean Sea. Also known as Saint Barts, Saint Barths, or Saint Barth, it is one of four Leeward Islands that comprise the French West Indies. It became an overseas collectivity (*collectivité d'outre-mer* or *COM*) of France on February 22, 2007. Previously it was a French commune of Guadeloupe, which is an overseas region (*région d'outre-mer*) and overseas department (*département d'outre-mer* or *DOM*) of France.

ICAO location identifiers are linked to the airport's Aeronautical Information Publication (AIP), which is available online in Portable Document Format (PDF) from the French *Service d'information aéronautique* (SIA).

Source (edited): "http://en.wikipedia.org/wiki/List_of_airports_in_Saint_Barth%C3%A9lemy"

F.D. Roosevelt Airport

F.D. Roosevelt Airport (IATA: **EUX**, ICAO: **TNCE**) is the airport located on the island of Saint Eustatius, Caribbean Netherlands. It was opened as "Golden Rock Airport" in 1946. Currently the only commercial aircraft that service the island are the DHC-6 Twin Otter and Britten-Norman Islander, although the runway can accommodate larger turboprop aircraft and some smaller jets. The airport has a small area for small aircraft. It has almost no terminal at all with no jetways or services.

The island is not a traditional Caribbean tourist destination and so it does not have the overcrowded beaches and blueprint resorts. The local government has however sought to increase tourism by attracting visitors to its world-class dive sites, hiking its dormant volcano The Quill and exploring the picturesque remains of its colonial history and its beautifully restored historic Oranjestad. Part of this plan is a proposed 1,000-foot (300 m) extension of the runway, in order to accommodate even larger aircraft and additional destinations.

Source (edited): "http://en.wikipedia.org/wiki/F.D._Roosevelt_Airport"

List of airports in Saint Pierre and Miquelon

This is a **list of airports in Saint Pierre and Miquelon**, sorted by location.

Saint Pierre and Miquelon is an overseas collectivity (French: *collectivité d'outre-mer*, or *COM*) of France, consisting of several small islands off the eastern coast of Canada near Newfoundland.

Airports

ICAO location identifiers are linked to each airport's Aeronautical Information Publication (AIP), which are available online in Portable Document Format (PDF) from the French *Service d'information aéronautique* (SIA).

Source (edited): "http://en.wikipedia.org/wiki/List_of_airports_in_Saint_Pierre_and_Miquelon"

Miquelon Airport

Landing at the Miquelon Airport May 15, 2008

Miquelon Airport, May 15, 2008

Check-in Desk at the Miquelon Airport

Miquelon Airport (French: *Aéroport de Miquelon*) (IATA: **MQC**, ICAO: **LFVM**) is a regional airport that serves the settlement of Miquelon in the commune (municipality) of Miquelon-Langlade, in the French overseas community (*collectivité d'outre-mer*) of Saint Pierre and Miquelon, off the eastern coast of Canada near Newfoundland.

The main building contains the check-in counters, control tower and fire fighting station.

There are no direct flights from France. Connecting flights to Paris are made via Montreal's Montréal-Pierre Elliott Trudeau International Airport.

The airport's runways are capable of handling turboprop or small jet aircraft only.

Source (edited): "http://en.wikipedia.org/wiki/Miquelon_Airport"

Saint-Pierre Airport

Saint-Pierre Airport from the road; May 14, 2008

Saint-Pierre Airfield from the airport; May 14, 2008

Saint-Pierre Airport (French: *Aéroport de Saint-Pierre*) (IATA: **FSP**, ICAO: **LFVP**) is a regional airport located 1 nautical mile (1.9 km) south of Saint-Pierre, in the French overseas community (*collectivité d'outre-mer*) of Saint-Pierre and Miquelon, off the eastern coast of Canada near Newfoundland.

The airport was completed in August 1999 and consists of four buildings and a control tower. The old airport, opened in 1965 and located on the south side of the inner harbour, was re-located due to the lack of room for expansion (The current runway is 1800m when compared to the old 10/29 at 1250m). The main terminal building is a two floor structure. The old airport is located in downtown St. Pierre and is being re-developed for housing. The control tower, terminal building, hangar and part of the old runway (mark number 29) are intact. The airport project cost 370 million French francs.

Facilities

- 2200 square metre passenger terminal
- 1600 square metre maintenance building to store snow plows
- 2500 square metre aircraft hangars and workshop
- 1400 square metre civil aviation buildings

The airport currently handles turboprop aircraft, but it can handle small jets up to a Boeing 737 or Airbus A319/Airbus A320

All other aircraft at the airport are private aircraft for general aviation.

There is only 1 scheduled airline operating from the airport.
Air Saint-Pierre Stephenville (NL) Charter service
Source (edited): "http://en.wikipedia.org/wiki/Saint-Pierre_Airport"

Argyle International Airport

Argyle International Airport is a future airport that is currently under construction in St. Vincent and the Grenadines. The groundbreaking took place in 2008, and the facility is expected to be completed by early 2012. The airport will cost around $240 million, and will replace the existing E.T. Joshua Airport, increasing passenger capacity by nearly four times compared to the older facility.

Overview

The island nation of Saint Vincent and the Grenadines recently realized that tourist, visitors and Vincentians find it a struggle to get to Saint Vincent, as they often have to get connecting flights to E.T. Joshua Airport through different islands, mainly Barbados (Grantley Adams International Airport), St. Lucia (Hewanorra International Airport) and Grenada (Maurice Bishop International Airport). Saint Vincent had ideas about expanding the E.T. Joshua Airport but soon realized that it would be extremely hard to extend the runways and building space. The two other sites that were recommended were Argyle on the eastern side of the island and Kitchen to the southeast. Eventually Argyle was decided upon to be the home of the new International Airport and work began on 13 August 2005. Many countries are helping with the building of the airport, including Cuba, Turkey, Iran, Taiwan, Trinidad and Tobago, Austria and Mexico. The runway is expected to be around 9,000 and feet long and 150 feet wide. A new date was also set for the opening of The Argyle International Airport date is set for March 2012.

For more information you can check out the International Airport Development company (IADC) http://svgiadc.com/index.asp The International Airport Development Company Limited (IADC)is a wholly owned government limited liability company, which was incorporated on 24 November 2004 under the Companies Act of 1994. The IADC is set up primarily to arrange the effective management of the completion of the international airport, and to secure its financing and construction at Argyle. The company is governed by an 11 member Board of Directors and is managed by a group of professionals headed by CEO Dr. Rudolph Matthias. The company is mandated to see the completion of the international airport at Argyle by the end of December 2011 and to begin training persons who would eventually manage the airport on its completion. The workers at the site are grouped under an umbrella called

Canouan Airport

Canouan Airport (IATA: **CIW**, ICAO: **TVSC**) is the airport located on the island of Canouan in Saint Vincent and the Grenadines. A land reclamation project and runway extension were completed at the end of March 2008. Overall runway length increased from 3,455 to 5,875 ft. This extension of the runway makes the airport accessible by a larger number of aircraft and can now accommodate aircraft from North and South America. Before the runway extension, the ATR 72 of American Eagle (Executive Airlines) was the largest aircraft to serve the airport. Currently, however, ATR service has been suspended pending runway certification and approval of night operations.

The airport has also just commissioned NDB/DME navigation equipment to complement the runway extension.

Source (edited): "http://en.wikipedia.org/wiki/Canouan_Airport"

E. T. Joshua Airport

E.T. Joshua Airport (IATA: **SVD**, ICAO: **TVSV**), also known as **Arnos Vale Airport**, is an airport located in Arnos Vale, near Kingstown, on Saint Vincent island. The airport was named for Ebenezer Theodore Joshua, the first chief minister of Saint Vincent and the Grenadines.

E. T. Joshua Airport will be eventually joined by a second airport at Argyle in St. Vincent named Argyle International Airport. The new airport is expected to be completed by 2012.
Saint Vincent's Argyle International Airport is expected to be completed by 2012.

Source (edited): "http://en.wikipedia.org/wiki/E._T._Joshua_Airport"

J. F. Mitchell Airport

J. F. Mitchell Airport (IATA: **BQU**, ICAO: **TVSB**) is the airport serving Bequia island, Grenadines Parish, Saint Vincent and the Grenadines, including Grenadines Parish' capital Port Elizabeth.

Source (edited): "http://en.wikipedia.org/wiki/J._F._Mitchell_Airport"

List of airports in Saint Vincent and the Grenadines

List of airports in Saint Vincent and the Grenadines, sorted by location.

Argyle(Just about 5.17 mile from Kingstown and 4.31 mile from E.T. Joshua Airport) Argyle International Airport under construction will replace the E.T. Joshua Airport sometime in March of 2012.

Source (edited): "http://en.wikipedia.org/wiki/List_of_airports_in_Saint_Vincent_and_the_Grenadines"

Mustique Airport

Mustique Airport (IATA: **MQS**, ICAO: **TVSM**) is located on Mustique island in Saint Vincent and the Grenadines.

Source (edited): "http://en.wikipedia.org/wiki/Mustique_Airport"

Union Island Airport

Union Island Airport (IATA: **UNI**, ICAO: **TVSU**) is the airport serving Union Island, Grenadines Parish, Saint Vincent and the Grenadines.

Source (edited): "http://en.wikipedia.org/wiki/Union_Island_Airport"

List of airports in Saint Martin

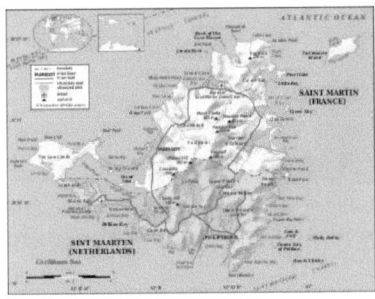

Map of Saint Martin/Sint Maarten with location of airports

This is a **list of airports in Saint Martin**, an island in the northeast Caribbean.

The southern Dutch half of the island comprises the *Sint Maarten* and is a constituent country. This portion contains the island's international airport: Princess Juliana International Airport.

The northern French half of the island comprises the *Collectivité de Saint-Martin* (Collectivity of Saint Martin), which became an overseas collectivity (*collectivité d'outre-mer* or *COM*) of France on February 22, 2007. Previously it was a French *commune* of Guadeloupe, which is an overseas region (*région d'outre-mer*) and overseas department (*département d'outre-mer* or *DOM*) of France. It contains the island's smaller airport which offers flights to the other islands of the French West Indies: Guadeloupe, Martinique and Saint Barthélemy.

Source (edited): "http://en.wikipedia.org/wiki/List_of_airports_in_Saint_Martin"

Princess Juliana International Airport

Princess Juliana International Airport (IATA: **SXM**, ICAO: **TNCM**) (also known as Sint Maarten International Airport) serves the Dutch part of the island of Saint Martin. In 2007, the airport handled 1,647,824 passengers and 103,650 aircraft movements. The airport serves as a hub for Windward Islands Airways and is the major gateway for the smaller Leeward Islands, including Anguilla, Saba, St. Barthélemy and St. Eustatius. It is named after Juliana of the Netherlands, who as crown princess landed here in 1944, the year after the airport opened. There is also an airport on the French side of the island near Marigot, called Aéroport de Grand Case or L'Espérance Airport.

History

The airport was started as a military airstrip in 1942. It was converted to a civilian airport in 1943. In 1964 the airport was remodeled and relocated, with a new terminal building and control tower. The facilities were upgraded in 1985 and 2001.

Modernisation

Because of increased passenger traffic and the expected growth of passenger traffic in the near future, Princess Juliana International Airport is being heavily modernized following a three-phased masterplan, commissioned in 1997.

Phase I was a short-term program in order to upgrade existing facilities and improve the level of service at various points. This included widening, strengthening and renovating the runway, increasing the bearing capacity of the taxiways, construction of a new apron and an upgrade of the (old) terminal. Phase I was completed in 2001.

Phase II included the construction of a radar facility and a new air traffic control tower, the construction of a new and more modern, 27,000 square metres (290,000 sq ft), terminal, capable of handling 2.5 million passengers per year, and the construction of a Runway End Safety Area (RESA) of 150 metres (490 ft), including a 60 metres (200 ft) overrun, on both ends of its runway, to comply with ICAO rules. The new air traffic control tower and the radar station commenced operations on March 29, 2004, while the new terminal opened in late October 2006. The terminal has 4-5 jetways for large aircraft like 747s.

If traffic develops as forecast, Phase III of the masterplan will be executed, consisting of an extension of the new terminal building and the construction of a full parallel taxiway system. The new terminal building will also have more jetways and services etc.

However, the oil price increases since 2003 began impacting discretionary air travel worldwide by early 2008, and the prospect of further price increases threatens to reverse the recent expansion of tourist travel by jet which began with the 1980s oil glut.

Runway and facilities

Video of Continental 757-300 landing at Juliana International Airport

Because the approach to Runway 10 is over water pilots can become disoriented regarding their perceived altitude when operating under visual flight rules. Normal instrument checks, coupled with experience and awareness, mitigate any potential problems. In fact, the departure from Runway 10 presents more "difficulties" than the approach, with a turn required to avoid mountains in the departure path.

Incoming airplanes approach the island on short final for Runway 10, following a 3° glide slope flying low over the famous Maho Beach. Pictures of low flying aircraft were published in several news magazines worldwide in early 2000. The thrilling approaches and ease of access for shooting spectacular images, made the airport one of the world's favorite places among planespotters. To meet changing international and local regulations a 150-metre (490 ft) safety extension was required.

Despite the reputed difficulties in approach, there have been no records of major incidents at the airport, though ALM Flight 980 crashed 30 miles from St. Croix on 2 May 1970, after several unsuccessful landing attempts at Sint Maarten-Juliana Airport (SXM - TNCM).

Towards the end of 2008, runway 09/27 has changed and now has a new QFU: 10/28.

Apron
The main apron measures 72,500 square metres (780,000 sq ft) with another 5,000 square metres (54,000 sq ft) on Eastern apron. For freight handling a dedicated apron of 7,000 square metres (75,000 sq ft) is available.

Terminal
The new 4 story terminal building offers 27,000 square metres (290,000 sq ft) floor space and is fully airconditioned. Available facilities include 42 check-in desks, 8 transit-desks and 11 boarding-gates. For arriving passengers 10 immigration booths are available and 5 emigration booths for departures. The building also features 40 shops and food & beverage units—some unique to St. Maarten—promoted under the retail theme 'So Much More'.

Private aviation
To accommodate the growing international and local traffic of private aircraft Princess Juliana International Airport has a Fixed Base Operators building, offering office space and private lounges with dedicated Customs.

Tower
Since official opening of the new control-tower PJIA Air Traffic Controllers have two radar systems at their disposal with a range of 50 nautical miles (93 km) and 250 nautical miles (460 km). PJIA air traffic control manages 4,000 square NM of airspace around the airport. Besides providing approach, tower and ground control at PJIA, Juliana air traffic services also provides approach control for Clayton J. Lloyd International Airport(Anguilla), L'Espérance Airport (St Martin, French West Indies), Gustaf III Airport (St. Barths, French West Indies), F.D. Roosevelt Airport (St. Eustatius) and Juancho E. Yrausquin Airport (Saba).

Navigation
PJIA is equipped with VOR/DME and NDB. The airport's official opening hours are from 07:00 - 21:00 hrs.

Joint border control with France
In 1994, the Kingdom of the Netherlands and France signed the Franco-Dutch treaty on Saint Martin border controls, which allows for joint Franco-Dutch border controls on so-called "risk flights". After some delay, the treaty was ratified in November 2006 in the Netherlands, and subsequently entered into force on 1 August 2007. Though the treaty is now in force, its provisions are not yet implemented as the working group specified in the treaty is not yet installed.

In popular culture
Princess Juliana International Airport is the airport featured in the free demo version of *Microsoft Flight Simulator X*. In the full version of the program, it is the destination on the mission called "Caribbean Landing". Princess Juliana International Airport is well known in the aviation world due to its popularity with aviation enthusiasts. Spectators are able to stand directly under the approach path to runway 10 as aircraft come in to land. There are also many YouTube videos of aircraft approaching the airport.

Gallery
Photos

A Piper PA-28 Cherokee light aircraft on short final for, at the time, Runway 09.

The new Terminal building from the inside.

Sign warning people that standing too close to the airport fence on Maho Beach can be dangerous.

Air France Airbus A340

Flight Schedule
Source (edited): "http://en.wikipedia.org/wiki/Princess_Juliana_International_Airport"

Andros Town International Airport

Andros Town Airport or **Andros Town International Airport** (IATA: **ASD**, ICAO: **MYAF**) is an airport serving Andros Town on Andros Island in the Bahamas. It is also known as **Fresh Creek Airport**.

It is one of three commercial airports on Andros Island. The airport is served by two airlines, but few tourists actually fly there. The airport is like any small Bahamian airport, with check-in, customs, gift shops and restaurants.

Facilities

The airport resides at an elevation of 5 feet (2 m) above mean sea level. It has one runway designated 09/27 with a asphalt surface measuring 1,237 by 30 metres (4,058 × 98 ft).
Source (edited): "http://en.wikipedia.org/wiki/Andros_Town_International_Airport"

Arthur's Town Airport

Arthur's Town Airport (IATA: **ATC**, ICAO: **MYCA**) is an airport in Arthur's Town on Cat Island in the Bahamas.

Charter flights

Aeroshares Charter, LLC services Cat Island from worldwide locations.
Charter service is also available from Florida or Nassau.
Source (edited): "http://en.wikipedia.org/wiki/Arthur%27s_Town_Airport"

Chub Cay International Airport

Chub Cay Airport is an airport in Chub Cay in the Berry Islands in Bahamas (IATA: **CCZ**, ICAO: **MYBC**). The airport actually lies in Frazers Hog Cay.
Source (edited): "http://en.wikipedia.org/wiki/Chub_Cay_International_Airport"

Clarence A. Bain Airport

Clarence A. Bain Airport (IATA: **MAY**, ICAO: **MYAB**) is an airport serving Mangrove Cay, part of Andros Island in The Bahamas.

Facilities

The airport resides at an elevation of 19 feet (6 m) above mean sea level. It has one runway designated 09/27 with a asphalt surface measuring 1,524 by 23 metres (5,000 × 75 ft).
Source (edited): "http://en.wikipedia.org/wiki/Clarence_A._Bain_Airport"

Colonel Hill Airport

Colonel Hill Airport (IATA: **CRI**, ICAO: **MYCI**), also known as **Crooked Island Airport**, is an airport in Colonel Hill on Crooked Island in the Bahamas.
Source (edited): "http://en.wikipedia.org/wiki/Colonel_Hill_Airport"

Congo Town Airport

Congo Town Airport (IATA: **COX**, ICAO: **MYAK**) is an airport near Congo Town in South Andros, part of Andros Island in The Bahamas. It is also known as **South Andros Airport** (IATA: **TZN**).

Facilities

The airport resides at an elevation of 15 feet (5 m) above mean sea level. It has one runway designated 10/28 with a asphalt surface measuring 1,623 by 30 metres (5,325 × 98 ft).
Source (edited): "http://en.wikipedia.org/wiki/Congo_Town_Airport"

Deadman's Cay Airport

Deadman's Cay Airport (IATA: **LGI**, ICAO: **MYLD**) is an airport located near Deadman's Cay on Long Island in The Bahamas.

Facilities

The airport resides at an elevation of 9 feet (3 m) above mean sea level. It has

one runway designated 09/27 with an asphalt surface measuring 4,000 by 100 feet (1,219 × 30 m).
Source (edited): "http://en.wikipedia.org/wiki/Deadman%27s_Cay_Airport"

Duncan Town Airport

Duncan Town Airport (IATA: **DCT**, ICAO: **MYRD**) is an airport located near Duncan Town, on Ragged Island in The Bahamas.

Facilities

The airport resides at an elevation of 6 feet (2 m) above mean sea level. It has one runway designated 13/31 with an asphalt surface measuring 3,800 by 75 feet (1,158 × 23 m).
Source (edited): "http://en.wikipedia.org/wiki/Duncan_Town_Airport"

Exuma International Airport

Exuma International Airport (IATA: **GGT**, ICAO: **MYEF**) is a public airport serving the island of Great Exuma in the Bahamas. It is located near Moss Town, northwest of George Town. The airport services mainly light aircraft and regional jets from the United States and The Bahamas.

Facilities

The airport resides at an elevation of 9 feet (3 m) above mean sea level. It has one runway designated 12/30 with an asphalt surface measuring 7,051 by 150 feet (2,149 × 46 m).

Airlines and destinations

The following airlines offer scheduled passenger service at Exuma International Airport:
Source (edited): "http://en.wikipedia.org/wiki/Exuma_International_Airport"

George Town Airport

George Town Airport (ICAO: **MYEG**) is an airport located near George Town on the island of Great Exuma in The Bahamas.

Facilities

The airport resides at an elevation of 5 feet (2 m) above mean sea level. It has one runway designated 11/29 with an asphalt surface measuring 5,000 by 90 feet (1,524 × 27 m).

Accidents and incidents

- On the 3rd of February 1998, Douglas C-47A N200MF of Missionary Flights International crashed on approach to George Town Airport. The aircraft was on a passenger flight from Cap-Haitien International Airport, Haiti when an engine failed shortly after take-off. The crew decided to return to George Town but the second engine failed on approach. All 26 on board survived.

Source (edited): "http://en.wikipedia.org/wiki/George_Town_Airport"

Governor's Harbour Airport

Governor's Harbour Airport is an airport in Governor's Harbour on Eleuthera in the Bahamas (IATA: **GHB**, ICAO: **MYEM**). It is the most active of the three airports on Eleuthera, and is about 8 miles north of the city.

Source (edited): "http://en.wikipedia.org/wiki/Governor%27s_Harbour_Airport"

Grand Bahama International Airport

Grand Bahama International Airport (GBIA) (IATA: **FPO**, ICAO: **MYGF**) is a privately owned joint venture between Hutchison Port Holdings (HPH) and The Port Group (or the Grand Bahama Port Authority). The facility also includes 741 acres of land that adjoins it to the Freeport Harbour Company Limited as they operate as one entity, known as the Sea Air Business Centre (SABC).

Grand Bahama International Airport is one of two Bahamian Airports that has US Border Pre-clearance facilities.

The airport has an 11,000 ft runway which is capable of handling the largest aircraft in service and is relatively close to all major cities of the Eastern Seaboard of the United States.

Some features that are available at the Grand Bahama International Airport are:

- ILS (Instrument Landing System)
- VOR System
- PAPI (Position Approach Path Indicator) system
- Distance Remaining Markers
- Category seven (7) Fire Fighting Facilities
- General Aviation services, including fuelling
- Special Cargo/Freight handling area
- US Pre-Clearance Facility

Accidents and incidents

- On 12 November 1964, Lockheed Lodestar N171Q stalled after take-off and was destroyed by fire in the subsequent crash, killing all four people on board.
- On 22 November 1966, de Havilland DH.125 N235KC of Florida Commuter Airlines crashed into the sea 7.3 kilometres (3.9 nmi) off Grand Bahamas during an illegal flight from Miami, Florida.
- On 24 November 1979, Convair 440-86 N444JM of Mackey International Airlines was on an international non-scheduled passenger flight to Fort Lauderdale International Airport when the starboard engine caught fire just after take-off. On approach to Grand Bahamas International, the engine fell off. On landing, the aircraft departed the runway and ended up in the sea. All 46 people on board escaped from the aircraft.
- On 12 September 1980, Douglas DC-3A N75KW of Florida Commuter Airlines, operating a scheduled international passenger flight from West Palm Beach International Airport, Palm Beach, Florida, United States to Grand Bahama International Airport crashed into the sea 6.5 kilometres (3.5 nmi) off West End. All 34 on board were killed.
- On 20 July 2000, Douglas C-47A N54AA of Allied Air Freight suffered an engine failure on take-off from Grand Bahama International Airport on a cargo flight to Nassau International Airport, Bahamas. The aircraft crashed while attempting to return to Grand Bahama International and was destroyed. Both crew were killed.

Source (edited): "http://en.wikipedia.org/wiki/Grand_Bahama_International_Airport"

Great Harbour Cay Airport

Great Harbour Cay Airport (IATA: **GHC**, ICAO: **MYBG**) is an airport serving Great Harbour Cay, one of the Berry Islands in The Bahamas.

Facilities

The airport resides at an elevation of 18 feet (5 m) above mean sea level. It has one runway designated 13/31 with a asphalt surface measuring 4,500 by 100 feet (1,372 × 30 m).

Source (edited): "http://en.wikipedia.org/wiki/Great_Harbour_Cay_Airport"

Inagua Airport

Inagua Airport (also known as **Matthew Town Airport**) is an airport in Matthew Town in Inagua in the Bahamas (IATA: **IGA**, ICAO: **MYIG**).

Source (edited): "http://en.wikipedia.org/wiki/Inagua_Airport"

List of airports in the Bahamas

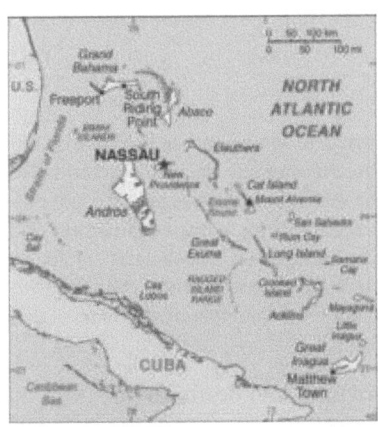
Map of the Bahamas

This is a **list of airports in the Bahamas**, grouped by island and sorted by location.

The Bahamas, officially the Commonwealth of The Bahamas, is an English-speaking country consisting of 29 islands, 661 cays, and 2,387 islets. It is located at the north-east of the Caribbean Sea in the Atlantic Ocean north of Cuba, Hispaniola (Dominican Republic and Haiti) and the Caribbean Sea, northwest of the Turks and Caicos Islands, and southeast of the United States of America (nearest to the state of Florida). Its total land area is almost 14,000 square kilometres (5,400 sq mi), with an estimated population of 330,000. Its capital is Nassau.

Airports

Airport names shown in **bold** indicate the airport has scheduled service on commercial airlines.

Source (edited): "http://en.wikipedia.org/wiki/List_of_airports_in_the_Bahamas"

Lynden Pindling International Airport

Lynden Pindling International Airport (IATA: **NAS**, ICAO: **MYNN**), formerly known as **Nassau International Airport**, is the largest airport in The Bahamas, and the largest international gateway into the country.

It is a major hub for Bahamasair and is located towards the west of New Providence island near the capital city of Nassau. Due to a large amount of flights to the United States, the airport contains U.S. Border preclearance facilities allowing all US flights to operate as domestic flights upon arrival at their destination.

The name of the airport was officially changed on July 6, 2006 in honor of The Right Honourable Sir Lynden Oscar Pindling (22 March 1930 – 25 August 2000), first Prime Minister of The Commonwealth of the Bahamas. Sir Lynden is hailed as the Father of the Nation, having led The Bahamas to Majority Rule in 1967 as well as Independence from the United Kingdom in 1973.

Expansion and renovations

Currently, the airport has 2 runways, more than 30 gates and 482,000 square feet (44,800 m) of terminal space. With more than 3 million passengers and 92,000 takeoffs and landings in 2008, the airport has reached its capacity and its facilities are outdated and insufficient.

In 2006, Nassau Airport Development Company (NAD) entered a 10-year management agreement with YVR Airport Services Ltd. (YVRAS) to manage, operate and redevelop the airport.

The redevelopment aims to update the airport facilities to world-class standards and expand terminal capacity. It will be carried out in three stages. The first stage includes the design and construction of a new 247,000-square-foot (22,900 m) U.S Departures Terminal. This stage is currently underway and has a budget of $198.1 million. Stage 2 consists of the complete renovation of the current U.S terminal, to serve as the new U.S/International Arrivals Terminal, with a budget of $127.9 million. Stage 3 involves the design and construction of a new 112,000-square-foot (10,400 m) domestic arrivals and departures terminal, as well as an International Departures Terminal at the location of the existing International Arrivals Hall. This last stage will cost $83.5 million.

Once complete, the $409.5 million invested will result in 585,000 square feet (54,300 m) of terminal space, a 21% increase, as well as the ability to accommodate 50% more passengers. It will also include the addition of 34 gates, including one capable of handling the Airbus A380. In all, this will provide the airport with a capacity to serve more than 5 million passengers annually.

The busy United States departures terminal at Lynden Pindling International Airport. More than half of the airport's international flights are to and from the United States.

Source (edited): "http://en.wikipedia.org/wiki/Lynden_Pindling_International_Airport"

Marsh Harbour Airport

Marsh Harbour Airport (IATA: **MHH**, ICAO: **MYAM**) is an airport serving Marsh Harbour, a town in the Abaco Islands in The Bahamas.

Marsh Harbour is a major tourist attraction in the Bahamas, it is home to just propeller aircraft and regional airliners. It serves Nassau and a few Florida cities. The government has been trying to expand the airport for years; groundwork has been started for a longer runway that could allow larger, regional jets to operate in and out of Marsh Harbour while the airport terminal has seen only minimal enhancements.

R&B Singer Aaliyah died in a plane crash on August 25, 2001 along with 8 others. The cause of the accident was the plane being overgrossed (overweight) making a successful takeoff impossible.

Facilities

The airport resides at an elevation of 6 feet (2 m) above mean sea level. It has one runway designated 09/27 with an asphalt surface measuring 1,523 by 30 metres (4,997 × 98 ft). As of December 2009, the old runway is being converted to a taxiway as the new 6,100 foot runway has opened. According to the Abaconian newspaper, the government is looking at the construction of a new terminal at Marsh Harbour to replace the current terminal, which is too small for the number of operators at that facility.

Airlines and destinations

Scheduled passenger service from this airport is provided by the following airlines:

Source (edited): "http://en.wikipedia.org/wiki/Marsh_Harbour_Airport"

Mayaguana Airport

Mayaguana Airport is an airport in Mayaguana in the Bahamas (IATA: **MYG**, ICAO: **MYMM**).
Source (edited): "http://en.wikipedia.org/wiki/Mayaguana_Airport"

New Bight Airport

New Bight Airport (IATA: **TBI**, ICAO: **MYCB**) is an airport in New Bight on Cat Island in The Bahamas.

Facilities
The airport resides at an elevation of 5 feet (2 m) above mean sea level. It has one runway designated 09/27 with an asphalt surface measuring 1,539 by 30 metres (5,049 × 98 ft).
Source (edited): "http://en.wikipedia.org/wiki/New_Bight_Airport"

Norman's Cay Airport

Norman's Cay Airport (IATA: **NMC**, ICAO: **MYEN**) is an airport serving Norman's Cay, one of the Exuma Islands in The Bahamas.

Facilities
The airport resides at an elevation of 8 feet (2 m) above mean sea level. It has one runway designated 03/21 with an asphalt surface measuring 3,000 by 60 feet (914 × 18 m).
Source (edited): "http://en.wikipedia.org/wiki/Norman%27s_Cay_Airport"

North Eleuthera Airport

North Eleuthera Airport is an airport in North Eleuthera on Eleuthera in the Bahamas (IATA: **ELH**, ICAO: **MYEH**). It serves the outlying islands of Harbour Island and Spanish Wells as well as the northernmost third of Eleuthera Island.
Source (edited): "http://en.wikipedia.org/wiki/North_Eleuthera_Airport"

Port Nelson Airport

Port Nelson Airport or **New Port Nelson Airport** (IATA: **RCY**, ICAO: **MYRP**) is an airport located near Port Nelson, on Rum Cay in The Bahamas.

Facilities
The airport resides at an elevation of 15 feet (5 m) above mean sea level. It has one runway designated 09/27 with an asphalt surface measuring 4,500 by 100 feet (1,372 × 30 m).
Source (edited): "http://en.wikipedia.org/wiki/Port_Nelson_Airport"

Rock Sound International Airport

Rock Sound International Airport is an airport at Rock Sound on Eleuthera in the Bahamas (IATA: **RSD**, ICAO: **MYER**).

Airlines and destinations
- Bahamasair (Governor's Harbour, Nassau)

Source (edited): "http://en.wikipedia.org/wiki/Rock_Sound_International_Airport"

San Andros Airport

San Andros Airport (IATA: **SAQ**, ICAO: **MYAN**) is an airport near Nicholls Town on Andros Island in The Bahamas.

Facilities
The airport resides at an elevation of 5 feet (2 m) above mean sea level. It has one runway designated 12/30 with a bitumen surface measuring 5,000 by 75 feet (1,524 × 23 m).

The airport has services from Westernair, Bahamasair, Lynx (from Fort Lauderdale) and other small twin engine charter planes that run between the islands.

Since November 2006, the airport has Av Gas and Jet A available from Westernair. The newly built Western Executive Jet Center has big screen TV, executive style bathrooms, conference rooms, pilot lounges, passenger area, delicatessen, and a VIP lounge. They also have a maintenance hangar for their aircraft and executive planes and a terminal for domestic flights.

Airlines and destinations

Scheduled passenger service from this airport is provided by the following airlines:

Source (edited): "http://en.wikipedia.org/wiki/San_Andros_Airport"

San Salvador Airport

San Salvador Airport (IATA: **ZSA**, ICAO: **MYSM**), also known as **Cockburn Town Airport**, is an airport in San Salvador, Bahamas.

San Salvador International Airport is one of the few airports in the Bahamas that has Instrument rating landing for airplanes, and as a result aircraft can now land at ZSA after official sunset (with local civil aviation permission).

Bahamas Customs and Immigration is present at ZSA between normal working hours of 9am-5pm. The main carrier at ZSA is the national flag carrier Bahamasair, which has daily flights to and from Nassau. Spirit Airlines flies into San Salvador Airport weekly out of its Fort Lauderdale hub. Club Med, a major hotel on the island, also has charter jet service flights direct from Paris, Montreal and New York.

Sky Bahamas Nassau

Accidents and incidents

- On 2 March 1973, Douglas C-47 N6574 of Arute International Air overran the runway on landing and was damaged beyond economic repair. The cause was pilot error in that a downwind landing was made. The aircraft was operating an international non-scheduled passenger flight from Miami International Airport, United States.

Source (edited): "http://en.wikipedia.org/wiki/San_Salvador_Airport"

Sandy Point Airport

Sandy Point Airport (ICAO: **MYAS**) is an airstrip serving Sandy Point on Abaco Island in The Bahamas.

Facilities

The airport resides at an elevation of 8 feet (2 m) above mean sea level. It has one runway designated 10/28 with an asphalt surface measuring 4,500 by 100 feet (1,372 × 30 m).

Source (edited): "http://en.wikipedia.org/wiki/Sandy_Point_Airport"

South Bimini Airport

South Bimini Airport is an airport in South Bimini on Bimini in the Bahamas (IATA: **BIM**, ICAO: **MYBS**). The airport was used as a staging point on the show Destination Truth.

Source (edited): "http://en.wikipedia.org/wiki/South_Bimini_Airport"

Spanish Cay Airport

Spanish Cay Airport (ICAO: **MYAX**) is an airstrip serving Spanish Cay, one of the Abaco Islands in The Bahamas.

Facilities

The airport resides at an elevation of 10 feet (3 m) above mean sea level. It has one runway designated 14/32 with a asphalt surface measuring 4,402 by 70 feet (1,342 × 21 m).

Source (edited): "http://en.wikipedia.org/wiki/Spanish_Cay_Airport"

Spring Point Airport

Spring Point Airport (IATA: **AXP**, ICAO: **MYAP**) is an airport serving Spring Point on Acklins Island in The Bahamas. Bahamasair flies to Spring Point Airport, and it is the only airline that flies here.

Facilities

The airport resides at an elevation of 11 feet (3 m) above mean sea level. It has one runway designated 13/31 with an asphalt surface measuring 1,524 by 46 metres (5,000 × 151 ft).
- Fuel: No Fuel
- Customs: No
- IFR: No
- Port Of Entry: No
- Authority: GOVT
- Contact: 242-344-3666

Source (edited): "http://en.wikipedia.org/wiki/Spring_Point_Airport"

Staniel Cay Airport

Staniel Cay Airport (IATA: **TYM**, ICAO: **MYES**) is an airport serving Staniel Cay, one of the Exuma Islands in The Bahamas.

Facilities
The airport resides at an elevation of 5 feet (2 m) above mean sea level. It has one runway designated 17/35 with a asphalt surface measuring 3,030 by 75 feet (924 × 23 m).
Source (edited): "http://en.wikipedia.org/wiki/Staniel_Cay_Airport"

Stella Maris Airport

Stella Maris Airport (IATA: **SML**, ICAO: **MYLS**) is an airport located near Stella Maris, on Long Island in The Bahamas.

Facilities
The airport resides at an elevation of 10 feet (3 m) above mean sea level. It has one runway designated 13/31 with an asphalt surface measuring 4,000 by 75 feet (1,219 × 23 m). The airport was designed and built by Jack Henry Cordery who was engaged by Stella Maris Estate Company in 1967 when he emigrated from England to take the job of Estate Development Manager. He died on Long Island in 1968 and is buried there.
Source (edited): "http://en.wikipedia.org/wiki/Stella_Maris_Airport"

Treasure Cay Airport

Treasure Cay Airport (IATA: **TCB**, ICAO: **MYAT**) is an airport serving Treasure Cay, in the Abaco Islands in The Bahamas.

Facilities
The airport resides at an elevation of 8 feet (2 m) above mean sea level. It has one runway designated 14/32 with an asphalt surface measuring 7,001 by 150 feet (2,134 × 46 m).
There is one terminal building, with departures in one room and arrivals in another. A small store sells snacks and the check-in desks are quiet if not crowded. No more than 15 planes arrive/depart a day, most to Florida and some to Nassau.
Source (edited): "http://en.wikipedia.org/wiki/Treasure_Cay_Airport"

West End Airport

West End Airport (IATA: **WTD**, ICAO: **MYGW**) is an airport that serves Grand Bahama. While smaller than the other airport on the island located in Freeport, this airport has two runways each 8,500 feet in length. This airport was recently re-opened and serves mostly cargo aircraft. The main runway is runway 10 and is the westernmost runway in the entire Bahamian archipelago.
Source (edited): "http://en.wikipedia.org/wiki/West_End_Airport"

Flamingo International Airport

Flamingo International Airport or **Bonaire International Airport** (IATA: **BON**, ICAO: **TNCB**) is an international airport located at Kralendijk, Bonaire, Netherlands. The Flamingo Airport serves as a connecting point for flights of KLM to some airports in South America. Thus airport once served as a hub for BonaireExel, BonaireExpress, CuraçaoExel, CuraçaoExpress, and it now serves the Dutch Antilles Express as its secondary hub, along with Insel Air, for its flights to and from Miami, Florida, and also EZAir serves Bonaire, as well as Curacao. as its main airline, although the airline itself is based at Curacao. The airport is also a refueling stop for KLM's flights to Ecuador.

Flamingo Airport is the third largest airport in the former Netherlands Antilles, behind St.Maarten's Princess Juliana International Airport and Curacao's Hato International Airport and is the fourth largest between the Caribbean islands of the Dutch Kingdom behind the already mentioned St. Maarten, Curaçao and Aruba's Queen Beatrix International Airport. Arkefly, Continental, Delta and KLM are currently the largest airline operators that operate scheduled flights to Bonaire.

The Flamingio Airport is large enough to accommodate most international wide-body airliners such as the Boeing 747, the Boeing 777, and the Airbus A340, although the largest wide-body type to operate to Bonaire today is the McDonnell Douglas MD-11, flown by KLM. This airport is used by medium-sized airliners such as the Boeing 727, Boeing 737, and Airbus A310.

History
Bonaire's first airport was located near

Tra'i Montaña Subi Blanku and walked across the current path of Kralendijk to Rincon. It was only a landing strip and a shelter. It was built in 1936 and is considered the place that is the beginning of aviation on Bonaire.

The construction work for this airport, began on September 23, 1935. The intention was to make a longer runway, but it proved impossible to see the more than 475 meters to make because the eastern portion of the land was very low. Part of the field had to be modified, in particular where the plane hitting the ground at the landing and rising. This area covered more than 100 metres from the runway which had to be paved with a mixture of sand and stone.

KLM decided on May 9, 1936, to take the risk to fly the first flight to Bonaire from Curaçao. The Oriol (Fokker F-XVIII "Snip"), was chosen for this test. The first experimental landing was successful and also a historic moment. Therefore KLM decided to make the first official flight with passengers and was scheduled to be performed on May 31, 1936.

American soldiers arrived on Bonaire in the second half of 1943 and their commander stated that a new airport had to be built. In December 1943, construction began in the vicinity of where the present airport now stands. The new airport, named "Flamingo Airport", was put into use in 1945. This was a big step forward for Bonaire and its aviation system. A small terminal was built that was suitable for the number of passengers at the time. This building was used until mid 1976.

The construction of a new runway began in the last months of 1953 and was completed in 1955. The small terminal had been extended with a terrace where luggage could be delivered. The runway was extended and expanded several times. In 1960, the runway had a length of 1430 meters and a width of 30 meters. Hotels and interested parties on the island continued to push for a further extension of the runway so that charter flights from the United States were able to land here. Those flights were often performed with DC8 or B707 aircraft.

In 1970, the runway was extended to 1750 meters long and 30 meters wide, enough for a DC9 to land and take-off with full load. On June 7, 1974, a public tender for the construction of a new terminal building was made. The building became operational in 1976. Meanwhile, hotels and foreign investors continued to insist that the runway be extended further. This was needed before any more hotels could be built. In 1980 the runway was again extended to 2400 meter long and 45 meters wide, and in 2000 another extension resulted in the current length of 2880 meter to facilitate the largest airliners on intercontinental flights.

The Dutch national carrier, KLM, started in 2000 using this airport to refuel planes en route from Amsterdam to Ecuador

Airport information and facilities

The first Bonaire-Miami flight took place on April 19, 1980, possible since the runway extension of that year. The current runway of 2880m is long enough for flights to Europe with a maximum take-off weight. KLM began with flights to Peru and later to Ecuador with a fuelstop on Bonaire in 2002. In recent years, the facilities at the airport have been modernized and expanded. There is a new departure hall, a new platform for wide body aircraft and a fuel farm was also added. As of 2009, Flamingo Airport is a full service stop for transit flights and the destination for many tourist flights, with air-conditioned offices, restaurant, departure hall and stores.

The airport registered a more than 10% increase in passengers in the first quarter of 2008. March was a record month and the increase has a lot to do with the Delta and Continental Airlines flights. Compared to the same period last year also the local passengers increased by 10.6%. International traffic increased by 8.8% which is breakthrough for the airport for Bonaire.

Since November 2005, visitors and tourists arrving at Bonaire are welcomed to a vibrant new Business and Tourism Showcase. A variety of colorful murals, vivid flat-panel displays, and high profile sponsored windsurfing sails will showcase all that the island of Bonaire has to offer. Pennsylvania-based Interspace Airport Advertising, through its subsidiary, Interspace Airport Advertising Curaçao, N.V., created the new terminal-wide advertising display program. Interspace will also manage the program through a 10-year partnership with the airport authority.

The airport has two main ramps. The smaller ramp, which is situated in front of the airport building. The ramp consist of 4 parking spots (PP1, PP2, PP3 and PP4) and is naimly used by smaller operating aircraft such as, DAE, Divi Divi, EZAir, Tiara Air and Insel Air, along with the larger Delta, Continental and Arkefly aircraft when the larger apron is in use by another large aircraft. The larger one is used for wide bodied aircraft such as KLM and Arkefly, but is also used by Continental Airlines, Delta and Insel Air, when vacant. The Larger ramp consist of two parking spots (PP5 and PP6). The management of the airport is currently working on the apron to allow two wide-bodied aircraft to park alongside each other, with the use of pushback cars, when ready for departure. At the beginning of the runway, lies the General Aviation's ramp, where mostly private aircraft are located. Due to overcrowding of the GA Ramp, some private aircraft utilize the larger ramp, at PP6 to park when overnighting and long stays.

In the past, the airport has been served by Air ABC, Air ALM, Air Aruba, Air Europe (Italy), Air Jamaica, American Eagle (Executive Airlines), Avensa, Avior Airlines, Bonaire Express/Curaçao Express (now Dutch Antilles Express), Canada 3000, Cats Air, Dutch Caribbean Airlines, Línea Turística Aereotuy, Martinair, Miami Air International, Royal Aruban Airlines, Servivensa, Sobelair and Surinam Airways.

BonAeroClub also offers sightseeing opportunities and also flight lessons with their Cessna 172.

Parking system and charges

Since May 2008, Bonaire International Airport (BIA) has started with the renovation of the parking places at Flamingo Airport. The airport introduces short- and long-term paid parking. Financial manager Gerard Chin-A-Lien indicated that the project will cost US$2.1 million. Most of this money will be spent on paving, installing the automatic parking system, landscaping, and lighting. This service official started on 5 September 2008. It is not possible to drop off passengers for free since August 2009 as you have to pay 1 guilder for the first 30 minutes and 1 guilder for each 30 minutes after that with a maximum of 20 guilders per day. Long parking costs 10 guilders per day. According to security manager Tico Wanga, a lot of attention is paid to safety with sufficient lights and cameras everywhere, and patrolling security personnel.

Check-in system and airport tax fee

In October 2008, Bonaire introduced the new CUTE system from SITA. CUTE stands for Common Use Terminal Equipment. This is a common use system whereby all airlines can use each of the 12 available check-in counters at Flamingo Airport. More flexibility is obtained while the processing capacity of passengers at the check-in counters is increased and made more efficient. The older check-in system worked with so-called dedicated check-in counters which were usable by only one particular airline and could not be used by other airlines, thus restricting processing capacity.

Due to the introduction of this new system, Bonaire International Airport N.V. will charge each departing passenger a service charge, starting December 1, 2008. This service charge amounts to 3.00 guilders (about US$1.69) and will be added to the existing passenger facility charge (airport tax).

Future plans

It is planned to expand the current airport building as more airlines and tourists come to Bonaire. It is also planned to expand the current departure and arrival hall of the airport to meet the standards of the amount of tourists that will be visiting the airport in the coming years and to repair the airport's runway after certain speculations that the runway had a crack in it. The Dutch Transport Minister, Camiel Eurlings, calculates that it will cost about €20 million (57 million guilders) to repair Bonaire's worn-out Flamingo International Airport runway. Since Bonaire is now the responsibility of the Netherlands, including ownership of the airport, it must comply with European standards, which are much stricter than the ICAO standards. Recently, the worldwide civil aviation authority conducted an audit on all of the airports within the Dutch Kingdom (including the rest of the Caribian parts of the Kingdom of the Netherlands) and said that they are just within standards. "Regarding the condition of the airport of Bonaire, there is no need to panic, there is no acute danger, only overdue maintenance. The runway needs heavy renovations and the people of Bonaire need a vital airport," concluded Eurlings.

The management of the airport is drawing up a master plan to comply with international requirements. There are three important projects planned which include:
- Maintenance of the runway (as mentioned above)
- Moving the fire station to the middle of the runway
- Purchasing two push-back cars for the heavy jets

Management is working very hard to make sure that Bonaire International Airport is as safe as possible and this way could welcome the aircraft that come to Bonaire and contribute to the growth of the tourism on the island.

Cargo services
- Ameriflight
- DHL Bonaire
- UPS
- Swissport

Other
- Netherlands Antilles & Aruba Coast Guard
- BonAeroClub

Note: The extrapolated data for 2008 are calculated without taking seasonal influences into account.
nyk: *not yet known*

Historical statistics
Between 2000 and 2003 the airport saw a ongoing grow in passengers and freight but some decline since 2004

Runway and approach
The single runway **10/28** is 2880 meter long and 45 m. wide. The actual heading is 92° or 272°. For runway 10 a *Simple Approach Landing System* is in place, for runway 28 no visual approach aids are available. Lighting of runway complies with all current regulations and back-up power system is available.

Reported/official runway-dimensions:
See for explanation of used terms article on Runway

Flamingo International Airport operates a Non-directional beacon on 321 KHz

General aviation facilities

Catering
Apart from the passenger terminal Bonaire Airport has facilities for freight and mail. Catering is available since *Goddard Catering* opened an airline kitchen on the island in 2003 offering complete airline catering. The Aruba kitchen uses ready-made imported frozen hot meals and locally made salads and appetizers.

Ground handling
Three local ground handlers operate at Bonaire airport.
- *Air Handling Service Bonaire*, which is the ground handling agent for DAE, Delta Air Lines, Insel Air and some cargo Services. It was also the agent for American Eagle before they discontinued their flights from and to San Juan. They also provide handling services to private jets.
- *Bonaire Air Services*, which is the ground handling agent for Air France-KLM, Continental Airlines and ArkeFly. It was also the agent for Air Jamaica prior to their discontinued flight to Bonaire.
- *Progressive Air Services*, which is the ground handling agent for Tiara Air and Kavok Airlines. *Progressive Air Services* also provides handling service to various private jets that

visit the island. It was also the ground handling agent for Transaven and Rainbow Air.
- *Swissport* also serves as one of the cargo and aircraft ground handling service on the island. *Swissport* was the ground handling agent for Arkefly (Curaçao), DAE (Curaçao) & Insel Air (Curaçao) before the handling of DAE & Insel Air has been later handled by *Air Handling Services Bonaire* and Arkefly is currently being handled by *Bonaire Air Services*.

Divi Divi Air & EZAir, are the only airlines with their own handling services and employees.

Fuel

Aviation Jet A1 fuel is available 24 hours a day via *Valero Bonaire Fuels Co N.V.*, owned by Valero Energy Corporation. On-site capacity of the tank-farm consists of two storage tanks of 630.000 gallons each. Every other week jet fuel is delivered to the island via a tanker from their own refinery at Aruba. *Valero* operates a direct pipeline from their landing-jetty to the airport. Two refueller trucks each with 15.000 gallons and one with 10.000 gallons are available.

Emergency equipment

The airport is categorized as *Fire Category 9* and on-site equipment includes 4 crashtenders and one rapid-intervention unit.

Incidents and accidents
- On October 14, 2009, a single-engined private plane, exploded in mid-air while flying over Bonaire. Witnesses near the west coast of the island witnessed a ball of fire falling from the sky at around 9pm. The bodies of the pilot and a passenger were recovered along with bales of drugs. The bodies, aircraft type and drug type have yet to be identified.
- On October 21, 2009, a Britten-Norman Islander BN-2A flight operated by local commuter airline, Divi Divi Air (registration: **PJ-SUN**), Flight 014 lost an engine while in flight to Bonaire and had ditch in the sea South-West of Klein Bonaire and five minutes out from Bonaire. Pilot Robert Mansell, 32, managed to successfully ditch the plane in the water but was knocked unconscious on impact. The passengers tried to undo his safety harness, but the plane was sinking too fast and he went down with the aircraft, but rescue boats managed to pick up all of the nine passengers that were on board.

Source (edited): "http://en.wikipedia.org/wiki/Flamingo_International_Airport"

List of airports in the Caribbean

List of airports in Caribbean.
The following categories contain lists of all Caribbean airports with Wikipedia articles:
- Category:Airports in Anguilla
- Category:Airports in Bermuda

Some Caribbean airports without articles can be found in the following manually-maintained lists:
List of airports in Anguilla, sorted by location.

Source (edited): "http://en.wikipedia.org/wiki/List_of_airports_in_the_Caribbean"

List of airports in the Netherlands Antilles

This is a **list of airports in the former Netherlands Antilles** upon its dissolution in 2010, sorted by location.

The Netherlands Antilles were part of the Lesser Antilles and consisted of two groups of islands in the Caribbean Sea: Bonaire and Curaçao (off the Venezuelan coast), and Saba, Sint Eustatius and Sint Maarten (located southeast of the Virgin Islands). The islands formed an autonomous part of the Kingdom of the Netherlands until the dissolution of the Netherlands Antilles in 2010.

Source (edited): "http://en.wikipedia.org/wiki/List_of_airports_in_the_Netherlands_Antilles"

List of busiest airports in Latin America by passenger traffic

Latinamerica 09 busiest airports by aircraft movements
Source (edited): "http://en.wikipedia.org/wiki/List_of_busiest_airports_in_Latin_America_by_passenger_traffic"

List of the busiest airports in South America

South America busiest airports by aircraft movements
Source (edited): "http://en.wikipedia.org/wiki/List_of_the_busiest_airports_in_South_America"

L'Espérance Airport

L'Espérance Airport (IATA: **SFG** / **CCE**, ICAO: **TFFG**), also known as **Grand Case Airport** (French: *Aérodrome de Grand-Case Espérance*), is a public use airport located in Grand Case, on the French side of the Caribbean island of Saint Martin. The airport is only used for smaller aircraft as Princess Juliana International Airport on the Dutch side of the island (known as Sint Maarten) is served by all major carriers.

Joint border control with the Kingdom of the Netherlands

In 1994, the Kingdom of the Netherlands and France signed the Franco-Dutch treaty on Saint Martin border controls, which allows for joint Franco-Dutch border controls on so-called "risk flights". After some delay, the treaty was ratified in November 2006 in the Netherlands, and subsequently entered into force on 1 August 2007. Though the treaty is now in force, its provisions are not yet implemented as the working group specified in the treaty is not yet installed.

Tower

Since official opening of the new control-tower PJIA Air Traffic Controllers have two radar systems at their disposal with a range of 50 nautical miles (93 km) and 250 nautical miles (460 km). PJIA air traffic control manages 4.000 square NM of airspace around the airport. Besides providing approach, tower and ground control at PJIA, Juliana air traffic services also provides approach control for Wallblake Airport(Anguilla), L'Esperance Airport (St Martin, French West Indies), Gustaf III Airport (St. Barths, French West Indies), F.D. Roosevelt Airport (St. Eustatius, Netherlands Antilles) and Juancho E. Yrausquin Airport (Saba, Netherlands Antilles).

Runway and facilities

Incoming airplanes approach the island on short final for Runway 12 over the bay of Grand-Case which is a tremendous view on final approach or when winds direction changes which is common incoming airplanes approach the island on short final for Runway 30 which is the opposite direction.

Larger aircrafts such as the ATR 72-500 powerbacks after lining up on the runway for departure due to the short runway.

The regional Esperance Airport at Grand Case allows the quickest transfers for commercial inter-island flights and for private aircraft (required to give a 24-hour notice to the Airport Authorities before landing).

Airlines and destinations

The following commercial airlines provide scheduled passenger service:
Source (edited): "http://en.wikipedia.org/wiki/L%27Esp%C3%A9rance_Airport"